A NEW HOLIDAY

TRAVEL GUIDE

SPAIN

The New Holiday Guide to

SPAIN

The New Holiday Travel Guide Series

M. Evans and Company   New York

Library of Congress Cataloging-in-Publication Data

The New Holiday guide to Spain.

  (The New Holiday travel guide series)
  New ed. of: The Holiday guide to Spain. Rev. and
updated ed. 1979.
  Includes index.
  1. Spain—Description and travel—1981-   —Guide-
books. I. Holiday (Philadelphia, Pa.) II. Holiday guide
to Spain. III. Series.
DP14.N47   1988   914.6′0483   87-5391

ISBN 0-87131-502-5

ISBN 0-87131-502-5
Manufactured in the United States of America
1 2 4 6 8 9 7 5 3
Revised First Edition

General Editor: Theodore Fischer

M. Evans and Company, Inc.
216 East 49 Street
New York, New York 10017

CONTENTS

CHAPTER 1

SPAIN: THE LAND AND ITS PEOPLE

"Europe," Napoleon said, "ends at the Pyrenees." His opinion may have been inspired by spite, since he learned about Spain the hard way. Nevertheless, his remark was accurate at the time.

The Iberian Peninsula is a geographic afterthought, some 650 by 600 miles in dimension, tagged on at the base of Europe and almost touching Africa at its southernmost point. It is sealed off on the land side by the bulwark of the Pyrenees, whose highest peaks average more than ten thousand feet, and by seas on the other three sides. The Pyrenean range is an effective insulator, as you will find if you cross the midsection of it. However, the border with France is easily crossed at each end of the range by the highways that run through Irún on the west and Port-Bou on the east. Major highways connect the principal cities and towns, good roads run through the hills and countryside, however some mountain roads can be tortuous.

Spain's tremendously varied coastline is named by sections. The **Cantabrian Coast** spans the entire north along the Atlantic with spectacular rocky and richly forested shoreline broken by *rías,* or fjords. This region is at its best during the summer months. The warm Mediterranean bathes the east coast, which is divided into six sections. From the French border to Barcelona, the *Costa Brava* (Rough Coast) has a jagged rocky shoreline dotted with hundreds of coves and sandy beaches. Heading southwards, the *Costa Dorada* (Golden Coast) becomes more fertile and flat. Valencia's *Costa del Azahar* (Orange Blossom Coast) is rich with orange orchards growing practically to the sea and lined with hills and endless stretches of flat sandy beaches. Along the Province of Alicante, the *Costa Blanca* (White Coast) is a continuation of rock outcrops and white sandy beaches that blend into stretches of dunes and virgin sand beaches. The *Costa Calida* (Warm Coast) boasts a sand spit that forms a natural breakwater and endless sandy beaches. Along the *Costa de Almería* undeveloped flat beaches rise into dramatic mountain slopes above crystal clear water. On the rim of mountains along Spain's southern Mediterranean coast, the *Costa del Sol* (Sun Coast) is lined with fine sandy beaches and a succession of resort towns. From Gibraltar to Portugal, the *Costa de la Luz* (Coast of Light) is an endless stretch of bright white sand beaches, dunes, and estuaries washed by the Atlantic surf.

Except to the Arab invaders, Spain has always been an uncommonly hard nut to crack. You will understand why when you see Spain, whether you arrive by air, land, or sea. Spain is mountainous. From the top of almost any pass you see ahead a steep descent into a valley, and across the valley the road winding upward again, twisting frantically to get out. And beyond the next crest another range, and beyond that another. (Only in the great central *meseta,* or plateau, of Castile will you travel on level ground, the mountains lying far off like blue ghosts.) Back and forth across the land the seven great ranges rule the country, most of them running east and west until they meet the coastal ranges that parallel the Mediterranean. But, as though this were not enough to dishearten the prospective conqueror—and to isolate the inhabitants —between the ranges flow the great rivers of Spain, not abundantly, but always broadly or in deep gorges.

Throughout most of their history the Spanish peoples—and there are many Spains in the Peninsula—have lived in isolation because of the terrain and have developed the attributes of individualism. Spain is a country of the *patria chica,* the "little native land." Ask anyone, *"¿De dónde eres?"* and he will answer, *"Burgos"* or *"Seville,"* meaning not even the province but the city. He is a separatist, eternally pulling away from the capital city.

The mountains do more: they deprive the interior of the rainy winds from the seas. Spain is dry. The rains fall chiefly in the north and northwest, on the seaward side of the ranges. Elsewhere, the rainfall is light and often tragically capricious. Along the central Ebro valley, for example, and in the valleys of the Jalón and the Guadiana, and in lower Aragón, violent storms (as often hail as rain) strike suddenly on the spring crops and the autumn harvests. The province of Albacete is the most parched of the interior Peninsula, with a rainfall as scant as two inches a year.

Certainly if you come to Spain for the sun, you will have it. In the Cantabrian area and in Galicia, of course, it is no torment, only an unpredictable visitor. Cádiz knows clouds, too, but nearly everywhere else the sun blazes daily through a clear, dry air. In the interior, the heat is brisk and stimulating for human beings, but it also causes swift evaporation of rivers, lakes, and lagoons, and of the water in the soil.

The Castle of Molina de Aragón in Guadalajara

Irrigation is practiced wherever possible—some of the canals and ditches you will see are centuries old—and there are dams and reservoirs all over the nation.

The sources of the people's income? Chiefly industry which employs almost half of the working population and thrives mainly in the areas of Madrid, Barcelona, Bilbao, Zaragoza, and Valencia. Agricultural pursuits, involving about one-quarter of the working population are the most obvious to the traveler; herds of the famed merino sheep originally brought over by the Arab invaders still graze on many a hillside, and, as the sun sets, farmers all over Spain return to their homes from a hard day in the fields.

As for mineral wealth, Spain's environment has been rich all through its history. The copper mines of the Río Tinto, near Huelva, and the mercury mines of Almadén have been among the world's greatest. Almadén mines have been worked since the 4th century B.C. and show no signs of exhaustion. The silver mines of the southeast, opened by the Phoenicians and deepened by the Carthaginians and Romans, produce enough today to rival Germany as a source of the metal. As for lead, Spain tops all Europe. Lignite, a low-grade coal, is abundant in Catalonia, and a slightly better grade is mined in Asturias, where there are also deposits of iron ore, so that the foundries of Bilbao carry some importance in the European market.

Then there is Spain's phenomenal hoard of salt. You will probably visit the splendid castle of Cardona, now a National Parador, northwest of Barcelona, and look out to a circular hill, three miles in circumference and five hundred feet high, glittering in the sun. It is a mountain of salt, an inexhaustible mountain that has been productive for more than twenty-five hundred years.

What are the Spanish people like? Generalizations about them can be dangerous and foolish, of course, yet there are certain traits that they themselves consider regional characteristics.

With the democratic constitution of 1978, the country began a gradual reorganization incorporating its 50 provinces into 17 Autonomous Communities: Andalucía, Aragón, Principado de Asturias, Islas Baleares, Canarias, Cantábria, Castilla-La Mancha, Castilla y León, Cataluña, Extremadura, Galicia, Comunidad de Madrid, Región de Murcia, Comunidad Floral de Navarra, La Rioja, Comunidad Valenciana, and País Vasco. In terms of personality and culture—and even ethnicity—Spaniards still tend to identify themselves and their land in terms of the ancient kingdoms or the individual provinces of their heritage.

The Catalán—who speaks a separate language and is very individualistic by nature—is said to be *muy listo,* quick and clever and extremely sharp in his dealings. He is the Yankee of Spain, cherishing as his hero *el gran caballero, don Dinero*—Sir Money. He has proved himself, in fact, an able man of business and of industry, the best in Spain. He is proud, reserved, and tight-fisted. Yet, he is excitable, he bristles with ideas and enterprises, welcomes intelligent innovation— and sometimes gets carried away. The region of Catalonia contains Spain's major port, Barcelona, and the Catalán works hard as businessman, exporter-importer, and manufacturer of textiles, shoes, hats, and specialized machinery. On the farm, by irrigation and endless labor he makes the obstinate land produce good yields. *Los catalanes de las piedras sacan panes,* they say—the Cataláns squeeze bread out of a stone.

The Cataláns' neighbor, the Aragonese, is held to be *muy duro y terquísimo*—very tough and extremely stubborn. He never gives in, he never gives out, he never gives up. The Aragonese are proud of the story of the burro from Aragón that wandered into Catalonia and started walking down a railway track. A Catalán express came toward him— and of course it was the train that backed up. The province of Aragón is so dry and infertile, so mountainous and hot, that only the very toughest human beings could survive in it. The man of Aragón is intensely loyal to family, to *patria chica,* and to one of the most ancient elements of his society, the church

The Navarrese is *muy noble*—very noble, very generous. His province, in Spanish terms, is green and fertile. Until a generation ago

Roman walls at Ávila

Galician farmer moving the family granary

thoroughly Basque-French, he has lately become more Spanish; nowadays you rarely hear the Basque language, Eúskara, spoken in the capital, Pamplona. Up in the mountains of Navarre, however, traces of the Visigoth still linger; the people tend to be blond, and many girls bear the old Byzantine-Visigothic name, Vasilisa, which means queen.

About the Basques of the Vascongadas it is particularly idle to generalize. Their land is green, they work it hard, they eat very well, they care about their traditions—but not even they know where their race came from. Their language is so difficult that, according to their own story, the Devil once tried to learn it by hiding behind the door of a Basque house, and came away seven years later with only a single phrase, "Yes, ma'am," a tribute to the women of the country. (The Basques glory in their impossible nomenclature, also. They like to tell you that the finest family name of their race is **BARRENE-CHEAGAMECHOGOICOECHEAITURRI.**) The Basques are notorious separatists, and the first Autonomous Community to be formed was the País Vasco.

Asturias is the Spanish Cradle of Independence. From here was launched the great Reconquest—the 800-year-long struggle by Christian Spain to oust the Arab invaders. At Covadonga, in the high Cantábrican mountains, you can still see the cave where the first few patriots gathered to begin the fight; it is usually crowded with visitors, like our Independence Hall. Today the Asturian girl is a beauty with an exquisite complexion. The male is tall among the men of the Peninsula, tends often to have Celtic blond hair and blue eyes, is a man of finished intelligence and discipline when educated, and rather uncontrollable when not.

Galicia is the Ireland of Spain, being Celtic with a tinge of Germanic stock. It is the wettest, least known and least visited of the provinces of Spain—and one of the most beautiful. Other Spaniards call the *Gallego* "sensual, melancholic, poetic, superstitious"—qualities he may have developed partly as a reaction to his country. Like the damp, poor Scotsman, the *Gallego* plays the *gaita,* a kind of bagpipe, of which he says, *"No canta, que llora"*—"it doesn't sing, it weeps."

Perhaps because of his barren environment, the *Gallego* leaves home oftener than other Spaniards. He is the porter, the load-carrier of the country; he is the itinerant harvester of its crops, following the season from south to north. And he is Spain's international man *par excellence;* he travels abroad frequently and stays a long time, but generally he returns to his *patria chica,* often well off, but sometimes as poor as when he left.

The people of the central plateau, the Leonese and the Castilian, share common characteristics except that the Leonese is held to be less stern. The Castilian is the mold out of which came the essential Spaniard of fact and fiction. The Castilian is grave when not stern, not much given to smiles or laughter, austere in manner and tradition, formidable in courtesy and kindness—whether countryman or grandee. He is the pre-eminent soldier of the Peninsula, and in the midst of the Spanish multitude of dissenters and separatists and individualists, he represents the one province disciplined enough to impose unity on the nation.

Moorish Andalucía, of which Extremadura, famed as "the land of the conquistadors," is sometimes considered akin, is the melting pot of the centuries. Andalucía is the first enlightenment of western Europe, brought by Phoenicians and Greeks and Romans. It is Cádiz on the Atlantic, a silver-and-blue city by which sailed the traffic of the New

A road, a stream, a field—and the mountains of León

World. It is Córdoba, seat of the Caliphate and of high learning. It is Seville with its centuries of Moorish splendor and culture. It is Granada and the glory of the Alhambra citadel, and it is the old Berber *taifa* of Málaga, said to possess *el alma de un jardin*—the soul of a garden. And it is the region that sent out most of the leaders and men who opened up the Spanish Empire: Valdivia, of Extremadura, who conquered Chile; Alvarado, of Seville, who explored and took Costa Rica and Guatemala; Pizarro, of Trujillo, who conquered Peru; Núñez de Balboa, of Jerez de los Caballeros, who discovered the Pacific; Cabeza de Vaca, of Jerez de la Frontera, who explored Florida, our own southwest, Uruguay, and the River Plate.

Andalucía is also the land of the barren steppes east of Úbeda and Granada, and of the spiny splendor of the Serranía de Ronda, and of the great Sierra Nevada and the African coast west of Almería. It is the richness of the valley of the Guadalquivir, as well as the barrenness of the gypsum-and-salt flats south of Ecija. (A Moslem, not a Castilian, said water was so scarce in Spain that it was cheaper to make mortar with wine.) It is vast olive orchards and vineyards and glowing fields of sunflowers. It is the hoary wealth of silver from Cartagena, of mercury from Almadén, of copper from the Río Tinto.

Andalucía is rich in romanticism and folklore. Its innate emotions of *alegría* and *tragedia* can be sensed through its flamenco music, song, and dance. It is the land of the great poet, Machado, and it still is saddened by the tragic death of its native son, García Lorca, another great poet, who was shot down brutally during the Civil War. The Spanish speak of life in Andalucía as a round of *sol, manzanilla y mujeres*—sun, manzanilla wine, and women. In springtime they compare the region to a *novia*—a girl betrothed. This is the land of spring flowers, of yellow broom and rock rose, tiny iris, valerian, peonies, and oleander. The iris in particular will cover a hillside so massively that the eye cannot determine where the slope ends and the sky begins.

Spain is a world in itself that begins at the Pyrenees and ends at Africa. It has ski slopes and sun-drenched beaches, and yet an even more varied mixture of peoples and cultures, all on one peninsula. As foreign as the Galicians may be to the Andaluces, and the Catalonians to the Castilians, they are all 100 percent Spanish.

CHAPTER *2*

THE BACKGROUND

In 1868 near Santander in northern Spain, a hound chased a fox into a small hole in a green hillside. The hound got itself stuck and its owner dug it free, and in so doing he exposed the opening of an enormous cave. Eleven years later a little girl, the daughter of an archaeologist, discovered pictures on the wall of a small chamber off the main cavern. They were the now famous Altamira paintings, dating from the Old Stone Age.

The bison, the deer, the horses, and the boar were done with crude materials—charcoal, ochre, red chalk, manganese ore—and the colors are limited to pale yellows, reds, browns, and black. But the paintings are skillful and extraordinarily life-like, revealing a sharper eye for anatomy than say, Giotto, had in Italy in the 14th century. Yet these pictures were drawn some 16,000 years ago.

In the Altamira Cave the history of Spain gets off to a visible beginning. There are other relics of prehistory: for instance, the Neolithic burial chambers that you can see throughout the Peninsula. The builders of these were the Iberians, who gave the land its name. They were a prehistoric race of long-heads, not very big of frame but powerful and energetic, who invaded Andalucía from North Africa, and brought commerce and industry to Spain. Their greatest achievement was Tartessos, the Biblical Tarshish, a fabulous city and empire whose culture led the western world of its day. Tartessos is first mentioned in 1200 B.C., and it may have been established in the tin trade as early as 2500 B.C. In any case, the city rose to be a golden legend, and its people masters of the strange seas beyond the Pillar of Hercules. Near Tartessos Homer placed the rivers of Hell. And here Hercules performed his Tenth Labor by stealing the oxen of the giant Geryon. Biblical accounts

Castle in Spain—at Torija, near Guadalajara

relate that "once in three years came the navy of Tarshish, bringing gold, and silver, ivory, apes and peacocks."

Next to invade Spain were the Celts, who began to trickle across the Pyrenees from western Germany and eastern France as early as 900 B.C. Three centuries later, drawn by reports of the plentiful tin, copper, and gold, they pushed en masse into the Spanish northwest, where they settled down in the valleys of the rugged mountains and preserved their own culture; into the west and southwest, where they mingled with other stock; and into the *Meseta Central,* where they amalgamated with the Iberians to produce the Celtiberian strain whom the Latin historian Florus called *robur Hispaniae*—the oak of Spain. They were conquerors by temperament, and by armament as well, for they carried terrible swords of iron.

Tough, intractible, and barbarous though the Celts were, they did little to disturb Tartessos or the smaller trading city of Gadir on a tiny peninsula opposite the metropolis. Gadir—the present Cádiz—was settled at the end of the Trojan War by the Phoenicians, who were the traders *par excellence* and suppliers of luxuries to all the ancient world. Tartessos was the richest market for Phoenician wares, and Gadir became the wealthiest, as well as the most remote, of their many colonies and trading posts throughout the length of the Mediterranean.

Another was Carthage, a flourishing settlement in North Africa. In time its people usurped the power of the ancient sailing masters and traders of Tartessos. Eventually they closed the Straits of Gibraltar, and the great Iberian city perished without a trace. (Many archaeologists have hunted for its ruins, but never a stone has turned up.)

When Rome emerged as a Mediterranean power, she inevitably challenged Carthage in the bitterly fought Punic Wars (264 B.C. to 146 B.C.), which ended with the complete destruction of the city of Carthage and its empire. But not before the Carthaginians under Hannibal had moved into Spain. Rome in turn dispatched armies against the Carthaginian forces; Roman Spain came into being.

But the Romans found they had to deal with a mountainous country and a people savagely independent, a trait they would never lose.

The war against two little cities, Numantia and Termantia, demonstrates the essence of Spanish resistance. At no time did the men of Numantia number more than eight thousand, while Termantia could not have put more than a few hundred in the field. And yet the campaign against them lasted twenty years and frustrated several Roman generals, one of whom surrendered twenty thousand Roman legionaries to four thousand Numantines. Numantia fell at last to Scipio Africanus, after he had built a wall entirely around the town and manned it for six months with sixty thousand men. Scipio got his triumph in Rome, and Numantia its moving memorial: *parva civitas sed gloria ingens*—a small city but immense in glory. It was burned and razed.

Roman amphitheater at Mérida

After the Peninsula was pacified, its people became Romanized at an extraordinary rate. They began to speak Latin, and to convert their towns into Roman municipalities. The Roman army was opened to Spaniards, and in the great period of the Empire two Spanish legions, the VIIth and Xth, became the most formidable trouble shooters of Rome.

In the time of peace the army was engaged in public works, and you can see their handiwork to this day. Hispalis and Italica (Seville) were built, and so were Caesar-Augustus (Zaragoza), Emerita Augusta (Mérida), Brigantium (La Coruña), and the superb, surviving city of Tarragona. Streets were paved; an excellent sewerage system was installed in towns such as Mérida and Barcelona; great cisterns for public water were built at Sagunto and Ampurias; aqueducts at Segovia, Mérida, and Tarragona; handsome public baths at Alange, near Mérida; public buildings such as the *curia,* or town hall, you may see —after a trip over a foul road, unfortunately—at Talavera la Vieja; theaters, amphitheaters, and circuses, like the magnificent theater at Mérida and the tremendous amphitheater at Italica, seating twenty thousand spectators; great arches like the ones at Medinaceli, bridges like that at Mérida, and, most overwhelming of all, that of Alcántara (Cáceres). And, as the chief implement of Roman rule and culture, the extraordinary network of the *vias Romanas*—eighteen thousand miles of principal highways driven across the plains and over the rugged mountains.

All this and more went into making Roman Spain and much came out of it. Trajan and Hadrian, two of the greatest Roman emperors, were Spanish, as was Marcus Aurelius. Spanish also were Quintilian the rhetorician, the younger Seneca, and many others important to the history of Rome.

By the beginning of the 5th century, the Roman empire began to fray along its edges. The barbarian Vandals, Alans, and Suebians piled ferociously through Spain, and the Vandals went spilling over into

Africa. Behind them came the Visigoths, in the year 414. Their kingdom endured for nearly three hundred years, but in that time they never acquired political wisdom and never, therefore, became colonizers in the Roman sense. Though they assimilated many of the Roman Spaniards' ways, when the North African Berber, Tarif ben Malluk, landed on the Spanish coast in 711, the Visigothic kingdom collapsed. A single pitched battle on the banks of the Guadalete, and the rulers became refugees hiding in caves in the impregnable Picos de Europa, far to the north, and in the mountainous tangle of Galicia.

Little trace of the Visigoths remains in Spain today: blond and red hair here and there in the Peninsula; a few Visigothic words in the vocabulary; and a certain sediment in Spanish law. Four of their lovely and humble churches have survived relatively intact, and it is well worth the drive out from Zamora to El Campillo to see the finest of these, San Pedro de la Nave.

It is hard to realize the meaning and effect of eight centuries of Moslem rule in Spain. All the years of Christian rule since the Moors surrendered their last bit of Spanish earth at Granada in 1492, add up to little more than half the period of Arab domination. And yet, throughout the Dark and Middle Ages, the Moslems in Spain showed the brightest and at times the only light in Europe.

Time and war have long since destroyed almost all the monumental evidence of the greatness of Moslem Spain. The three principal structures left, however—the Mosque at Córdoba, the Alhambra at Granada, and the Giralda tower at Seville—are among the architectural wonders of western Europe. What is far more important—and often forgotten—is that out of Moslem Spain came the original intellectual enlightenment of medieval Europe.

The process goes back to one Abd-er-Rahman, who declared himself Emir of Córdoba in the middle of the 8th century and established a centralized power throughout Moslem Spain. The six emirs of his line who followed him during the next century consolidated Arab power and held at bay the Christian kings who pressed toward the Reconquest.

One of the greatest of these emirs was Abd-er-Rahman III, who came to power in 912 and ultimately declared himself Caliph of Córdoba and Commander of the Faithful. Under him Córdoba entered a century of extraordinary splendor during which western Europe sat at its feet to learn and admire and copy. A nun from remote Saxony wrote after seeing Córdoba that it was "the ornament of the world . . . young and exquisite, proud of its strength . . . radiant." The man responsible for this brilliance, Abd-er-Rahman III, was one of the greatest figures Europe had seen since the collapse of Rome.

Under his son, Al Hakam (961–976), the Córdoban Caliphate saw its most peaceful and brilliant days. The new Caliph was a highly cultivated man, a patron of letters and sciences, and a bibliophile—his

Columns and arches of the Mosque at Córdoba

library contained 400,000 volumes, at a time when the monastic librar-
ies of Europe numbered their tomes in the dozens and secured them
with chains. The kings of Europe and the East sent unnumbered emis-
saries to the fabulous mile-long palace of Az-Zahara, built by his father
just outside the walls of Córdoba.

Córdoba indeed became the Bagdad of the west, the home and
vitalizing center of old knowledge forgotten elsewhere and of new
knowledge that medieval Europe had not yet discovered. In Córdoba,
and only there, were found the dedicated and trained philosophers,
historians, grammarians, and astronomers. It was Córdoba that attracted the geographers who introduced the works of Ptolemy to
Europe. Within its walls (still Roman), pharmacology, and botany
were transformed into formal sciences. Plane and spherical trigonome-
try were conceived there. In Córdoba the astrolabe and other instru-
ments of science were developed. There, too, the surgeon Abulcasis
wrote a medico-surgical encyclopedia that was translated into Latin,
Provençal, and Hebrew, and influenced European surgery and medi-

cine for centuries. With its university (and twenty-three free schools for poor children), the city grew into a seething center of learning and art.

At the death of Al-Hakam, Abu Amir Mohammed ibn Abí Amir became the Grand Vizier of the Caliphate, and in the year 981 adopted the name by which he is known in history—Almanzor, "The Victorious." It is no exaggeration to say that this man struck like a flash of lightning through the history of his time. The Christian Reconquest was literally paralyzed by him. He fought his first campaign the year after Al-Hakam's death. From then until his own death a quarter of a century later, he lost not a single battle. His name alone, running ahead of his army, could empty a Christian province three days before his arrival. Once he planted his standard on a hill outside Burgos and departed; it remained there undisturbed for days because no one dared to leave the city and verify his absence. After each campaign Almanzor would shake the dust out of his robes and have it stored in a small chest he carried with him. In the year 1002 he fell ill of an epidemic, was carried to Medinaceli, his favorite city in Castile, and there died. He and his little chest of triumphant dust lie buried somewhere on one of the many hills that rise in the stark landscape beneath the high rock of Medinaceli.

After the death of Almanzor, however, the Caliphate of the west fell apart, and the Reconquest was able to drive south once more, free of terror for the first time in two hundred years. Toledo fell in 1085. Islamic strength was shattered at the battle of Navas de Tolosa in 1212, and within thirty years the Christians established themselves from the Atlantic to the Mediterranean in a half-circle close about the small kingdom of Granada.

Even with the Reconquest all but complete, violent dissension among the Christian kingdoms made Spanish unity impossible. Then, in 1366, Henry II, called Henry of Trastamara, became king of Castile, and his line stretched out, sometimes well, sometimes ill, until at last

Covadonga, the Asturian cave where the Reconquest began

it produced Queen Isabella, a sovereign as great in Spanish history as Elizabeth I was in English. Under Isabella and her husband Ferdinand, Spain emerged from medievalism, was unified, and made ready for her great future. Isabella was crowned queen in 1475. In 1492 her Castilian herald stood below the walls of Granada and proclaimed the final departure of the Moslem from Spain. And in the same year Columbus sailed from Palos de la Frontera. These three remarkable people came together at a decisive point in history, and all helped to create the Spanish empire.

With the reign of *los Reyes Católicos,* the "Catholic Kings," as they are called, Spain re-enters the stream of European history. Isabella died in 1504, spending her last hours drawing up a new codification of the laws of the realm, leaving orders that the Indians of her new empire be treated humanely and never be enslaved, and issuing instructions that her body be taken to Granada, the scene of her great conquest. She lies there still, and in the light of her talents and accomplishments, her plain lead coffin is a deeply moving sight.

In a grimly contrasting context, the reign of Isabella also saw the Spanish Inquisition launch its hunt for heretics, in what was to become the most brutal religious persecution until the blood baths of the present century. Since the Middle Ages, the light of religious persecution had flared all over Europe, set ablaze not only by the Catholics but also by the Calvinists of Geneva and the churchmen of Scotland; it flickered even in the New World at Salem, though no burnings took place there.

In Spain, persecution of Jew and Moor rose to its climax in the 16th and 17th centuries. The number of people brought to book can only be estimated now. It is known that, from 1500 to 1525, 348,907 *Marranos* —converted Jews accused of practicing Judiasm occultly—were tried; 28,540 condemned to death and some 12,000 burned at the stake. Nor was the bloody business confined to non-Christians; some of those who had trouble with the Holy Office were later canonized, among them St. Teresa of Ávila and St. Ignatius Loyola. The excesses of the Spanish Inquisition have been especially well-chronicled, compared to the reporting of similar activities in other European countries.

The Inquisition was finally abolished at the beginning of the Carlist War, in 1833. It is only fair to add that in Spain the institution had operated almost independently, and that its excesses have not always been condoned by the Church. Still, after centuries of fanatic persecution, the Inquisition emerged without a drop of blood on its hands. Thousands were condemned to the stake and the garroting post to purify their souls, but technically the Inquisition executed no one. Its victims were, in the words of the formula, "released to the secular arm." It was the state that did the killing.

After Isabella, the Empire was well under way. Charles I—better known as Charles V of the Hapsburg Empire—came to the throne of Spain in 1516. While those extraordinary men, the Conquistadores, built up an enormous realm for him in the New World, Charles extended his sway in Europe, fighting religious and political wars in Germany and wars of rivalry with France. In the process he poured out the gold of the New World and spent the tough soldiers of Spain—for generations the foremost infantrymen of Europe. He squandered even more men and money as Emperor of Germany, which he became in 1529, than as King of Spain. The most conspicuous man of his century, he had gained great glory and prestige by 1556, when he retired from the throne to his modest quarters at Yuste monastery. He had also nearly bankrupted his kingdom.

With the 42-year reign of Philip II, Charles' son, the fortunes of Spain began their downhill course. Philip's bastard half-brother, the famous soldier, Don Juan of Austria, did win a brilliant and significant victory against the encroaching Turks, at the sea battle of Lepanto. Elsewhere, however, Philip poured out his physical and financial resources in desperately useless intervention in the religion and politics of Europe. Revolts against his fanatic rule boiled up constantly in the Low Countries. The French under Henry IV defeated him and most calamitous of all, in an expedition against England he lost his invincible Armada.

Under Philip III, the decay of Spain became unmistakable. He shared his father's bigotry, but he lacked both the ability and the conscience to govern his kingdom, and turned the reins over to his favorite, the corrupt and incompetent Duke of Lerma. The king intervened in Spanish affairs once only, and then stupidly: in 1609 he expelled nearly a million *moriscos*—descendants of the Spanish Moslems who remained in Spain after the fall of Granada—who were his most skillful and industrious subjects.

When Philip IV succeeded his father in 1621, the prestige of the crown was still high and its European possessions practically intact.

The bay at San Sebastián

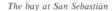

The Escorial, Philip II's Royal Monastery

Like his father, the new Philip turned over the management of royal affairs to a favorite, the Duke of Olivares, but he proved to be an able and conscientious statesman, though blundering at times. Yet had he been twice as able, and had he not had the ill luck to be matched against Richelieu in France, he still could have done little to check the decline of his country's greatness. By Philip's death, in 1665, Spain had lost most of its extra-Peninsular territory in Europe. Yet all during his reign, and the earlier reign of Philip III, the Golden Age of Spanish art and literature was at its zenith. The names of Cervantes, Calderón, Lope de Vega, Góngora, Velásquez, Zurbarán, El Greco, and Murillo are all bright flowers that bloomed in the decay.

The successor to Philip IV, Charles II, struck the final dismal note. He was the scrag-end of the Hapsburgs, the last of them to rule Spain —a pathetic, sickly, imbecilic, prematurely senescent creature known as the Patient King. Yet poor Charles, who died in the first year of the 18th century, did one good thing. By willing his "twenty-two crowns" to the Duke of Anjou, the grandson of Louis XIV and great-grandson of Philip III—an act which touched off the thirteen-year War of the Spanish Succession—he placed on the throne the first of the Spanish Bourbon line. The Duke, recognized finally as Philip V, behaved always as a man of conscience, principles, and peace. It was largely his doing that started Spain on its century of slow recovery from the Hapsburg slump.

Under the two Bourbon kings who followed him, Ferdinand VI and Charles III, Spain enjoyed a long enlightenment, a period limited by the Bourbon concept of benevolent despotism, but nevertheless productive of many intellectual, political, and scientific advances. The enlightenment continued even under the ineffectual Charles IV, thanks to one Manuel de Godoy, chief minister to the King and notorious lover of the Queen. Godoy died in exile, much hated by the people, yet during his ascendancy he did much to improve the intellectual and political climate of Spain.

In the midst of Spain's slow comeback, Napoleon appeared on the scene, and Spain was drawn into the long conflict, first with, and then against, him. The Franco-Spanish fleet was destroyed by the British at Trafalgar in 1805. Three years later Napoleon invaded Spain and established his brother Joseph on the throne. The resistance that followed, known in Spain as the War of Independence, was a gallant and desperate guerrilla action against the finest troops of Europe. It took four hard years of fighting and considerable assistance from the British under Wellington, but eventually the French were driven out.

Free now of outside oppression, Spain floundered in internal strife. The issue was the new liberalism versus the archaic absolute power of the crown. The reactionary Ferdinand VII sat on the throne supposedly under a liberal constitution written in 1812. Before his death in 1833, however, Ferdinand designated his infant daughter, Isabella II, to be his heir, thus offending his even more reactionary brother Charles, who claimed the throne, and precipitating the Carlist War. In the next forty years Spain lived through a chaos of governments, monarchs, dictators, and even the short-lived First Republic of 1873–74. Then Isabella's son Alfonso was invited to return as king, and he in turn was followed by a son, who came to the throne as Alfonso XIII. This was the ruler who allowed General Primo de Rivera to become dictator in 1923, and who finally, in 1931, after a general election that was a sweeping victory for the Republican-Socialist Party, quietly left Madrid forever, the only Bourbon ever to give up a throne without bloodshed.

Sadly, the change came too late. No reform, not even Alfonso's tardy abdication, could mend the breach in Spain, a country that had learned only lately to accept unity, and then only as something imposed. The new republican government began the task of political and economic reforms hopefully enough. Soon it was wavering before attacks by both

Street scene, Canena

the liberal and the conservative opposition. In 1934, occurred the revolt of the Asturian miners—who had leftist support—and the government signalled its preference for the policies of the right. Two years later the Popular Front—an uneasy coalition of republicans, Socialists, syndicalists, and Communists—won a resounding victory at the polls. It was a tragic victory, because it triggered off the bloody Civil War of 1936–39.

The rebel forces—whose ranks included monarchists, clericalists, landowners, and industrialists, as well as dissident army officers and arch-conservative Carlists from Navarre—erupted out of Spanish Morocco under General Francisco Franco. Swiftly they organized around the core of the army and the Fascist Falange. Soon they were receiving substantial military aid from both Germany and Italy, while the legal government, denied assistance from the democracies by the ineffectual "nonintervention" policy of these countries, was bolstered only by a trickle of supplies from the U.S.S.R. and muddled help from liberal and leftist groups elsewhere. The war exploded with shocking violence and blazed on with Spanish tenacity, month after tortured month, until at last—nearly three years and a million lives later—the government forces surrendered in March, 1939.

In the even greater devastation of World War II, the new corporate Spain preserved a precarious and somewhat suspect neutrality. After the collapse of Fascist states, the Franco regime managed, in spite of open hostility from victorious western democracies, to stay in power.

The nation remained politically and economically ostracized until 1953 when the United States obtained the right to establish military bases there in exchange for economic aid. Two years later, Spain was admitted to the United Nations. Even so, Franco kept the country under very tight control until the early seventies when a combination of failing health and actively hostile public opinion forced him to give way to a timid liberalization.

Franco died in 1975, thus bringing to an end 40 years of dictatorship. Democracy was smoothly restored with the accession to the Spanish throne of King Juan Carlos I de Borbón y Borbón. The monarch, as Head of State, is assisted by the President of the Government and the Council of Ministers. A democratically-elected Cortes drafted the present Constitution, ratified in 1978, defining the country as a democratic state governed by a parliamentary monarchy with legalized political parties.

Between 1980 and 1982, the regions of Catalonia, the Basque Country, Galicia, and Andalusia passed their own Autonomy Statues and elected their own parliaments. Subsequently the rest of the country was organized into 17 "Autonomous Communities," one of which was Madrid, seat of the national government.

Internationally, Spain has joined NATO and has been admitted to the European Economic Community (EEO), thus strengthening ties with the rest of Western Europe.

CHAPTER 3

WHAT YOU SHOULD KNOW ABOUT SPAIN

A FEW PRELIMINARIES

Passport and Visa. You'll need a passport. To obtain a Passport Application, contact the Passport Agency in Boston, Chicago, Detroit, Honolulu, Houston, Los Angeles, Miami, New Orleans, New York, Philadelphia, San Francisco, Seattle, Stamford, or Washington; one of the many Federal or State courts; or a U.S. Post Office that accepts passport applications. You must present proof of citizenship, two 2× 2-inch square photographs, color or black & white, and a fee of $35 (plus a $7 processing fee when applying in person) for adults ($20 + $7 for minors). No visa is required for U.S. or Canadian passport holders for a stay of up to six months. To remain longer than six months, a special visa from the Consulate of Spain is required before your departure. The address of the Consulate General of Spain in New York is: 150 East 58th Street, New York, NY 10155; 212-355-4080. Other Spanish consulates in the U.S. are located in: Boston, Chicago, Houston, Los Angeles, Miami, New Orleans, San Francisco, and Washington, D.C. In Canada, the Consulate of Spain is located at 199 McAllister, Toronto, Ont.; 416-636-1216.

Medical. Spain requires no inoculations, and smallpox vaccination is no longer required for re-entry into the United States.

Spanish meals, especially lunch *(comida)* and dinner *(cena),* are much more extensive in variety and quantity than what you are probably accustomed to, and there are many more between-meal snacking opportunities. Many dishes are prepared with olive oil. You might experience some gastrointestinal changes, therefore, moderation for the first few days is recommended.

Columns of the Court of the Lions, the Alhambra

Customs. Customs procedures have been simplified in Spain. Some import restrictions apply to tobacco and liquor; photographic, sporting, and electronic equipment and supplies should be for personal use. You won't have any problems unless your luggage is loaded with them. Spanish customs officials are most polite and, as anywhere, courtesy begets courtesy. Theoretically, one movie camera and two still cameras are allowed per person, with ten rolls of film for each. Film is readily available in the larger cities, but it is still wise to take your own supply with you. Spain is pre-eminently photogenic. So take more film than you can possibly need. You'll use it all.

Getting to Spain. Most travelers fly directly to Spain. In addition to a range of airfares to choose from, tour operators and the airlines themselves offer a wide variety of fly/drive, escorted, and independent tour packages. A knowledgeable travel agent, airline offices, and the National Tourist Office of Spain can provide brochures and information and assist you with your plans and itinerary.

By Air: Iberia Airlines of Spain offers nonstop service to Madrid from New York (daily), Los Angeles, Chicago, Miami, and Montreal. Iberia also flies nonstop from New York to Málaga (Costa del Sol), Tenerife (Canary Islands), and, during the summer, to Santiago de Compostela (Galicia). TWA offers connections from cities throughout the United States to daily New York-Madrid nonstops. Aeroméxico flies nonstops between Miami and Madrid. Spantax, a Spanish charter airline, flies between New York and Spain at economical fares.

There is a vast range of airfares, depending upon the class of service and season. The lowest fares are in effect during the low season, from January 1 to March 31; mid-season fares apply from April 1 to May 31 and August 16 to October 31; peak season is from June 1 to August 15. A money-saving APEX mid-week winter New York-Madrid

The Cathedral at Salamanca

roundtrip fare can be as low as $449, while a first class roundtrip, valid for one year with no restrictions, costs $3,540.

If you would like to combine your trip to Spain with other countries in Europe, Spain's major European gateways include Barcelona, Madrid, Málaga, Palma de Mallorca, Santiago de Compostela, Seville, Valencia, and the Canary Islands. Excellent connections are also available to Africa and the Middle East.

Domestic flights on Iberia or Aviaco connect major cities. A shuttle service (Puente Aereo) runs hourly between Madrid and Barcelona from early morning until late evening.

A Car in Spain. There are many options for renting a car in Spain. The super highways are excellent, and the out-of-the-way country roads offer delightful sightseeing and close-up views of picturesque villages and towns. Many package tours include car rentals at various destinations as well as fly-drive combinations. Iberia and TWA often feature special car rental promotions which sometimes include a free self-drive car in conjunction with transatlantic airfare or a tour package.

Hertz, Avis, and the Spanish company Atesa are among the biggest in Spain, with locations all over the country and at major airports.

Hertz provides "Computerized Driving Directions" at no additional charge as well as *European Driving Tours,* a book with suggested one-week driving tours complete with detailed itineraries, maps, suggested routes, and a sightseeing gazetteer.

The Avis "Personally Yours" customized travel planning service is offered free on the Costa del Sol and on Mallorca. It provides a detailed driving itinerary designed with tour stops from eight categories: Highlights of Spain, Undiscovered Spain, History of Spain, Castles & Palaces, Antiques, Parks & Gardens, Museums, and Shopping & Crafts.

Atesa, the largest Spanish car rental company, has counters at all major airports. It offers a full range of late model vehicles, from economic subcompacts to chauffeur-driven luxury sedans. The "Free One-Way Privileges" service allows you to drop off your car at any of its locations. You can book Atesa car rentals through their general agent in the United States, Marsans International Tours. Marsans also offers an attractive selection of travel programs and packages to Spain. Contact one of their U.S. offices: 205 East 42 St., New York, NY 10017 (212-661-6565); 1680 Michigan Ave., Miami Beach, FL 33139 (305 531-0444); or 3325 Wilshire Blvd., Los Angeles, CA 90010 (213-738-8016). Or, you can call their toll-free number in your area: Northeast and Midwest, 800-223-6114; Southeast states, 800-544-4454; West Coast states, 800-525-8495; Florida, 800 432-1056; California, 800-525-5515.

For more flexibility, you might wait to rent your car once you are in Spain or rent a car with an English-speaking driver-guide.

Car rentals in Europe are not cheap by U.S. standards. Whether calculated on an unlimited mileage basis, or time plus mileage, a straight rental of a subcompact (group A), such as a Ford Fiesta or a Seat Panda (Seat is the Spanish version of the Fiat), costs approximately $32 per day and under $100 per week. Keep in mind that rates should include unlimited public liability, property damage, and fire and theft insurance. Be prepared to pay an additional 12% value added tax (VAT).

An International Drivers License is required and may be obtained from branches of the American Automobile Association. The minimum driving age in Spain is 18.

Speed limits are 60 kpm. (37 mph.) in cities, 90 kph. (56 mph.) on country roads, 100 kph. (62 mph.) on national roads, and 120 kph. (75 mph.) on highways. Keep in mind that traffic police are very strict in Spain, and they *do not* take bribes. Wear seat belts outside city limits, use turn signals, and don't blow the horn in cities.

About maps. The Michelin road maps are excellent. Distribution of these in Spain is uncertain during the tourist season, so it is wise to get them before you leave. The Spanish Ministry of Transportation, Tourism and Communications also publishes excellent road maps as does Campsa, the Spanish Petroleum Company.

Planning. Even though the point has been labored in every guide since Marco Polo's time, it should be said again that sensible planning is essential. The more you know about the country you are going to see and about how you are going to use your time while you are there, the more enjoyable the trip will be. The preliminary preparations can be a pleasant prelude, and they are sure to yield dividends.

The National Tourist Office of Spain will, of course, happily provide much useful and current information, brochures, and advice. In the United States they have offices at: 665 Fifth Ave., New York, NY 10022 (212-759-8822); 845 N. Michigan Ave., Chicago, IL 60611 (312-944-0215); 8383 Wilshire Blvd., Beverly Hills, CA 90211 (213-658-7188); 5085 Westheimer, Houston, TX 77056 (713-840-7411); Casa del Hidalgo, Hypolita & St. George Streets, St. Augustine, FL 32084 (904-829-6460). In Canada: 60 Bloor St. West, Toronto, Ontario M4W-3B8 (416-961-3131).

Note: *1992—the Fifth Centennial.* Spain is going all out to celebrate the 500th Anniversary of the Discovery of America, on Columbus Day, October 12, 1992. Seville is preparing for its Expo '92, which will transform the city in to what is claimed will be the most important World Exposition ever to take place on the planet. Simultaneously, Barcelona is excitedly getting ready for the 1992 Summer Olympics to be held for the first time in Spain. If you are interested in visiting Spain for either of those events, start making your plans and reservations soon!

The Weather. The climate of Spain defies generalization. It is safe to say that Spain is at its best and brightest during May and again during

October. The sun will be warm and pleasant, the nights, cool. You may occasionally have to reach for your raincoat to ward off cool winds, especially the moisture-laden ones along the Atlantic. During daylight savings time, the summer sun doesn't set until around 10:30 P.M., allowing bonus hours for sightseeing.

The bare and very general meteorological facts, subject to the usual vagaries, are these:

Central Spain, where the sky is almost always brilliantly bright, tends toward extremes, hot in summer, cold in winter. But in Madrid, because of its altitude and dryness, both heat and cold are usually bracing.

The northern Cantabrian Coast drizzles in winter and becomes a resort area during the summer.

The Mediterranean coast is largely subtropical, hot in the interior, cooler along the coast itself. Valencia has a suave climate, almost never without sun. Barcelona can be muggy in mid-summer, but it is still a delightful city. The Balearic islands are damp in December and January, but a paradise for lotus-eaters for the rest of the year.

Clothing to Take. Because of the variations in the weather, it is difficult to prescribe exactly what kind of clothes you will need. Generally, in winter, you will use warm, wind-proof and waterproof clothing—unless you are on the Mediterranean coast. In spring and autumn, modify this, but stand by for occasional sharp winds and fresh nights; this means a sweater and a light coat.

Attitudes towards clothing have changed a good deal in Spain over the last few years. The wearing of slacks by women is no longer frowned upon, and bikinis can be worn on the beach without causing a scandal even in the most out-of-the-way fishing village. In fact, in many ultra-cosmopolitan resorts along the Costa del Sol, and in places such as Mallorca and Ibiza, the women, as well as the men, go topless. Nevertheless, the general dress code should be that of respectability and good taste.

Valley of Riaño, a National Park in León

HOTELS

In Spain you can stay on the Mediterranean in a luxurious, modern hotel, or you can spend a few nights in a castle that was slept in by kings. And there are plenty of accommodations in between.

You will find a general listing of hotels in the *Fact Finder,* beginning on page 114.

National Paradors *(Paradores Nacionales).* Spain is known for its incomparable ancient castles, palaces, monasteries, convents, and hospices. A great many of them have been meticulously restored, and all modern facilities and amenities have been installed. These are the superb government-owned and operated National Paradors. Many more have been built in recent times, designed either to blend in architecturally with a historical town or site, as a modern hotel whose location was chosen for its historical, cultural, or scenic importance, or for its attractiveness as a beach or mountain resort area. Many are situated in areas where no other accommodations exist, thus enabling travellers to explore places they may not otherwise have the opportunity to visit. More than 80 Paradors are located throughout Spain and visitors can easily design an itinerary through all of Spain, or to certain regions, staying at Paradors along the way. They feature the regional dishes of their location as well as fine international cuisine, and the service is always outstanding. The interior decor usually follows regional themes and often includes museum-piece antiques, handicrafts, and invaluable works of art.

The Paradors are classified into four-, three-, and two-star categories. The rates vary according to season, but are comparable to those of the hotels in the same star category. Understandably, accommodations at the Paradors are very much in demand, so it is advisable to make reservations well in advance. For information, rates, and reservations, contact the representative of the National Paradors in North America:

Virgen de la Cabeza, the parador at Andujar

The Roman aqueduct at Segovia

Marketing Ahead, Inc., 433 Fifth Avenue, New York, NY 10016 (212-686-9213). You can also obtain brochures, but not reservations, from the National Tourist Office of Spain.

Once you have signed in at your hotel, you must turn over your passport to the *conserje,* the concierge, who will fill out a police registration form and then return it to you in short order. If, however, you plan to leave at an "early" hour (to be explained shortly), it is wise to request that the passport be returned to you that same night. This is a common procedure in Europe. It doubtless causes the local bureaucracies some extra work—but for the individual it can be a useful record. Should you lose your passport or have it stolen, the number is registered with the police.

Language Note. In deluxe and first-class hotels and restaurants you will find that English is spoken almost as a matter of course. In fact, English has replaced French as the required second language in schools in most of Spain. Like other Europeans, Spaniards are proficient in foreign languages. And since you are in their country, some serious attempt to learn a basic Spanish vocabulary will prove to be rewarding. (A brief guide to the language is included in this book.) Regardless of how much Spanish you know, you're liable to be totally flabbergasted when you hear some Spaniards talk and you don't understand even a syllable. They could be speaking Galician *(gallego),* Catalonian *(catalán),* Valencian, or even Basque *(euskera).* Although they are required to speak, read, and write Castillian Spanish, it could well be their second language.

Since Catalonia became an Autonomous Community, Catalán replaced Castillian Spanish as the official language. Signs and most street names are in Catalán, and some universities require students from other parts of Spain to pass their exams in Catalán. Catalonians may prefer to converse with tourists in English rather than in Castillian, even though they all speak it well.

Hours. Lunch, called *la comida,* is the main meal of the day. Preceded by *tapas* (Spanish appetizers), it takes place from at least 2 P.M. to 4 P.M. and is longer and later on weekends. Shops and stores are usually open from 9:00 A.M. to 1:00 or 2:00 P.M. and 5:00 to 7:30 P.M., Mondays through Fridays, and open mornings only on Saturdays. The "morning" in Spain does not end at noon, but rather at *comida* time, and the afternoon begins thereafter. Major department stores, such as El Corte Inglés and Galerías Preciados, with branches all over the country, remain open at midday and stay open late on Saturdays.

Standard bank hours are 9:00 A.M. to 2:00 P.M. Monday through Friday, and some are open 9:00 A.M. to 1:00 P.M. Saturdays. Some currency exchange windows may be open from 5:00 to 7:00 P.M. Currency exchange booths at international terminals of major airports have hours that coincide with international flights.

Standard business hours are 9:00 A.M. to 2:00 P.M. and 4:30 to 8:00 P.M.. Some companies are changing to a nine-to-five schedule, much to the dismay of the traditionalists. In the cities, dinner, or *cena* is between 9:00 P.M. and midnight, and the nightlife just begins to get started after midnight.

Theater performances begin at 10:00 or 11:00 P.M.; movies begin earlier.

Most museums remain open all day, Tuesdays through Sundays, and are closed on Mondays. Churches and convents which may also be museums usually close at midday, although cathedrals remain open. The smaller and more fascinating the country village churches, the more likely they are to be closed when you want to see them; you just have to ask around.

Dining room in the National Parador Duques de Cardona in Catalonia

Maid Service. The average hotel maid will see to your laundry, your dry cleaning, and keep your room in tip-top shape.

The Concierge. This official is the factotum of the Spanish hotel. A polite approach on your part, assuring him that his services are superb and indispensable will make your path smooth. He handles your passport matters, sells you stamps, mails your letters, accepts and pays for packages delivered for you, sends out for oddments or repairs you need, buys your theater and bullfight tickets, and is your most reliable source of information in the hotel.

CURRENCY

You may buy pesetas on this side and take them with you into Spain. There is no limit on the amount of foreign currency you bring in. Here as within Spain the rate of exchange is about 130 pesetas to the dollar as this guide goes to press. Upon leaving Spain, you can take out the equivalent of 500,000 pesetas in foreign money not exchanged, and up to 100,000 pesetas in Spanish currency. All other forms of currency (checks, travelers checks, etc.) may be brought out in unlimited amounts.

It is only ordinary prudence not to carry more money with you than you can afford to lose. The safest and most convenient way to carry the bulk of your funds is in traveler's checks. Those issued by American Express and other international banking firms are readily accepted throughout the country.

For most Americans, either American Express in Madrid and their affiliated offices in other cities, as well as any Spanish bank with an exchange *(cambio)* sign in its window, are the places to change your money at the going rate with a minimum of fuss and delay, although there is a small service charge. The hotels do *not* usually give you the going rate.

The *peseta,* the Spanish monetary unit, is pronounced peh-SET-ah. (Don't embarass yourself by calling it a *peso*). Coins that are primarily in circulation are in denominations of 1, 5, 25, 50, 100, and 200 pesetas; bills are in denominations of 200, 500, 1,000, 2,000, 5,000, and the newly-issued 10,000 peseta bill.

Check your first pocketful of change to become accustomed to identifying coins, as some are similar and most have the same profile of King Juan Carlos I on the head side. The 100-peseta coin, with a faint copper tinge, is about the same diameter as a U.S. quarter and twice as thick. It is easily confused with the five-peseta coin (nicknamed *"duro"*), which is only slightly smaller, and also with the slightly larger 25-peseta coin. (You might come across some *céntimos,* of which there are 100 to the peseta, but they are obsolete).

TIPS

This troublesome problem has fewer rough edges to it, perhaps, in Spain than in some other countries. Your hotel bill includes an extra 15 per cent for service. Nevertheless, if maid, bellboy, doorman, or concierge have done something special for you, you will probably acknowledge it with an extra present. You might remember that in Spain the official minimum wage is lower than in the U.S., and that most of the servants in the hotels earn less than you would think.

Even though a 15% service charge is included in a restaurant bill, if the food and service are good, a small tip or 5% or more is expected.

This is a good place to speak of tips in general:

In *tapa* bars, *cafeterías,* and taverns, your change will always be delivered in a little dish. If it includes a couple of *duros,* leave them on the plate, even though you will receive a friendly "Gracias, hasta luego" whether you do or not.

To the man who carried your baggage: 50 to 100 pesetas per piece.

Taxi drivers don't expect tips but a few *duros* will be appreciated. If it is a substantial ride, tip about 10%.

For a friendly service done you by a passerby on the street, a clerk in a store, or a man out in the country—nothing but your best thanks and a smile or a handshake. You can insult a Spaniard by trying to reward him with money for help that he is proud to give you.

GETTING ABOUT IN SPAIN

It is one thing to say that in Spain the main roads are excellent, though a bit narrow, and that the secondary roads are apt to be suspect. The troublesome fact is that you can't tell what sort of road you're about to deal with merely by noting its color on your road map. A road that last year was calculated to reduce your car to a whimpering scrap heap may now be opened up, fine and smooth as silk. To be on the safe side, check with your car rental agency or a local tourist information office, and carry an up-to-date road map.

You can be sure of two things: 1) that the roads are much better now than they have been since Roman times; 2) that many rare and beautiful sights are at the end of pock-marked, dusty roads. Spanish superhighways are as good as any in Europe, and the lesser roads, for the most part, are very well maintained.

Driving your own car will, of course, give you greater freedom of movement, and in recent years both gasoline supplies and the number of service stations has greatly increased.

Busses. Service is available throughout Spain at very reasonable rates, slightly lower than train travel. Busses travel to many towns not accessible by train and are also good for short trips, such as the 44-mile ride between Madrid and Toledo. Quite apart from public busses are the tour busses, called *autocars.* They are extremely luxurious, air conditioned, and often equipped with TV and VCRs.

Taxis. They are inexpensive all over Spain. The cars are maintained in top condition and the drivers are highly reliable. A light on the roof and a *"libre"* sign in the window means the taxi is for hire. In Madrid the meter starts at 80 pesetas (about 65¢) and an average downtown ride costs around $3.00. There is a 150-peseta supplement to go to the airport and 50-peseta supplement late at night and on Sundays. Suburban and out-of-town trips have special fares. Barcelona is divided into taxi zones, and the fares vary accordingly. In some cities there are cars called *"gran turismos"* that don't have taxi meters. Their fares are higher, and it is advisable to ask in advance what the fare will be.

Rail Travel. RENFE, the acronym for *Red Nacional de los Ferrocariles Españoles,* or the Spanish National Railway Network, has expanded and improved its facilities and service throughout the country. It offers several classes of service to major cities as well as small towns, plus connections to international rail lines.

Trains enter Spain from France at Perpignan-Figueres, on the Mediterranean side of the "isthmus" of the peninsula, and at Biarritz-San Sebastián on the Atlantic side. Express trains from Paris to Madrid or Barcelona leave every evening and arrive in the morning.

The best Spanish trains are the ultra-modern Talgos, which have sleepers, "couchettes," and first- and second-class accommodations. Also excellent are the luxurious "Electrotrenes". The misnamed "Expreso" and the "Rápido" are slower.

Spain's new "Tourist Trains" are a unique concept in sightseeing excursions. Operated by RENFE, each train is named after a special destination and makes a one-day or weekend excursion out of Madrid during the spring, summer, and fall months. All have hostesses on board and the trips include guided tours and other activities. *El Tren de la Fresa,* "The Strawberry Train," is a restored 19th-century train that leaves from Madrid's National Railroad Museum and takes passengers, attended by hostesses in period costumes serving strawberries, to Aranjuez (famous for its strawberry crops) for lunch and a visit to the Royal Palace. The others are *electrotrenes: Las Murallas de Ávila,* "The Walls of Ávila," makes a scenic tour of the ancient walled city. The *Doncel de Sigüenza* is named for the legendary page *(doncel)* of

Washday—by a 2000-year-old Roman Bridge in Salamanca

Part of the city of Jaén

the City of Sigüenza. *La Plaza de Salamanca* visits the city of Salamanca which, in its entirety, has been declared a national monument and is famous for its magnificent main square. And the *Ciudad Monumental de Cáceres* makes a weekend trip to the monumental city in the Region of Extremadura which has been declared a Cultural World Heritage Site by UNESCO. Subsidized by the regional tourist boards, the one-day packages cost under $10 and the weekend excursions are similarly inexpensive. Advance reservations and tickets can be obtained at any RENFE office in Spain.

Eurailpass, which offers unlimited bargain train travel during a set period of time, and must be purchased before leaving for Europe, is also honored in Spain.

In addition to RENFE's other discount fares, their "Tourist Card" program is ideal for visitors who want to travel unlimited kilometers in Spain for a modest price. It is available to any traveler whose permanent residence is outside of Spain. It can be purchased for periods of 8, 15, or 22 days of unlimited travel for approximately $108, $175, and $208 respectively for first class, and $75, $125, and $158 for second class. The "Tourist Card" can be purchased at any of RENFE's offices throughout Spain, including the ones at the Irún and Port-Bou stations on the French border, and at RENFE's office in France: 3 Avenue Marceau, 75016 Paris (47.23.52.00).

The *Al-Andalus Express,* one of Europe's most luxurious trains, is actually a 5-star "gran luxe" hotel on wheels that travels through Andalucía (Seville, Córdoba, Granada, Málaga, and Jerez de la Frontera) on a 4 ½-day roundtrip itinerary that includes on-board dining, entertainment, and excursions. Marsans International, previously mentioned, can provide information, brochures, and reservations.

By Boat. You can travel around coastal Spain on board the ferry boats and cruise ships of Transmediterranea. You can take inter-island trips in the Balearics in the Mediterranean and the Canaries in the Atlantic, and combine them with cruises to or from Barcelona, Valencia, Málaga, and the Costa del Sol and Cádiz on Costa de la Luz. Marsans International is also the general agent for Transmediterranea.

By Air. Iberia, together with Aviaco (Spain's domestic airline), operate a wide network of flights between the major mainland and island cities. For travelers who *really* want to get around, Iberia offers a unique Visit Spain Airpass for air travel in Spain during any 60-day period throughout the year. For $199 the traveler can choose from as many as 30 destinations served by Iberia and/or Aviaco. And for an extra $50 the "Airpass" includes six of the Canary Islands. The Airpass must be purchased prior to departure from the U.S. and in conjunction with Iberia transatlantic service. Discounts for children and infants are 50% and 90% respectively.

FOOD & WINE

There are a few things you must know about Spanish food.

Spanish food is not Mexican. It is our southern cousins who burn out your piping—appetizingly, it must be admitted—with violent peppers. The most characteristic Spanish seasoning for rice dishes is saffron. It is not at all heating, although the Mediterraneans for centuries have hoped that it is aphrodisiac, and it is considered the world's most expensive spice.

Spanish cooking is not French. Butter is available, but not in the kitchen. There it is olive oil—not inferior to butter, but different. And the meals made with it are gigantic.

Garlic is much admired in Spain. There's no rubbing a small clove of it lightly over bowl or meat. The Spaniard holds it to be the Pierian spring of flavor. He knows that it's good for teeth and hair—in which his nation is conspicuous—and, probably, that it soothes and regulates the child. Larger hotels and restaurants aim at being French, and you'll not be troubled by garlic there. But elsewhere simply ask the waiter to tell the cook not to include it in your dish.

Pork, well done in all provinces—though they sometimes serve it with sugar in Galicia—is always on hand. Roast suckling pig, *cochinillo,* is superb; also, baby lamb chops, *chuletillas,* a dozen to a plate, the nut of meat on each not larger than the first joint of your thumb, and much tastier.

Throughout central and north Spain, one used to find the authentic

Sitges beach, near Barcelona

Castilian dish called the *cocido*, or the *olla podrida*, a vegetable-and-meat stew that relied heavily upon the chick pea, potatoes, and cabbage. It was a one-dish meal: the broth, for a soup; the chick peas next; then the meat on its platter, surrounded by the other vegetables.

Throughout the country, although more expertly along the Mediterranean coast, much is made of the rice dish called *arroz paella*: with meat or chicken, or, as in the *paella valenciana*, with every kind of shellfish, nicely decorated with strips of red pepper.

Gazpacho is a soup that should be eaten in Andalucia. To retain its racial purity, it must contain garlic, olive oil, wine vinegar, raw minced cucumbers and tomatoes, and bread crumbs—and anything else as long as it is vegetable, minced and raw. Served cold, it's an extraordinarily refreshing dish on a broiling hot day.

In the Basque Country, which is reckoned to offer the best cooking in Spain, the good and unusual dishes to be tried are the codfish *en casserolle*, called *bacalao a la vizcaína*, and the baby eels *en casserolle*, simply called *angulas*. These last are about half an inch long, and you eat thousands of them at a sitting. Here in the north, as well as along the Mediterranean, you will also find that familiar specialty, baby octopus in its own ink, *calamares en su tinta*, which, despite its appearance, is a delicacy.

The fish of the northwest, living in the icy waters of a tail of the Labrador Current, are probably the most savory of the Northern Hemisphere. Fast trucks bring these fish into the center of Spain, on ice. In fact, Madrid, with its colossal consumption of seafood, is often called "one of Spain's biggest seaports." So try the northwestern version of

Cathedral tower in Valencia   *Gaudi's 'Sagrada Familia' in Barcelona*

the lamprey, *lamprea;* the shad, *saboga;* the European hake, *merluza;* and the red mullet, *salmonete.* Add the shellfish, *mariscos:* the big crayfish and the shrimp, *langostino* and *gambas,* which absolutely require icy water for texture and taste; the clam, *almeja;* the crab, *cangrejo,* especially the spider form; the oddly delicious goose barnacle, *percebe;* and the succulent mussel, *mejillón.*

The Catalán dishes, of course, run to fish: *sopa de pescado,* a delicious fish soup, especially at "Solé," on the water front in Barcelona; *suquet,* a fish chowder, the Catalán form of bouillabaisse; *salmonete,* the mullet, grilled, with a sprinkling of garlic, fennel, and parsley; *sardinas,* at their best from May to August; *bogavantes,* the genuine lobster, best around Cadaqués and Calella, on the Costa Brava; *niu,* slices of cod *en casserole* with squab and potatoes; and *embutidos,* sausages.

Two other dishes will be found everywhere in the country: the *flan,* an egg custard, very good; and the *tortilla española,* a potato omelette, which will see you through the roughest and longest day.

Wines. Spanish wines are stronger than French wines. They have their own personality, are very palatable and relatively inexpensive. Among the most popular are: Paternina, *cepa Borgona, banda roja* (red band); Paternina, *cepa Borgona, banda azul* (blue band); Marqués de Murrieta, *gran reserva;* Bodegas Bilbaínas, their "Pomal"; and Rioja Alta with their *Gran Reserva* 904 and *Viña Arana.* Well-known white wines *(blanco)* are: Marqués de Murrieta, *gran reserva;* Paternina, *cepa Rhin* —a Rhine-wine type; López Heredia, their "Tondonia"; and Franco-Españolas, their "Monopole." Also, try "Viña Paceta" and "Viña Diamante" (white), both from the Rioja, the river banks of the upper Ebro, where most of the good wine is made.

Out in the provinces you will do well to try the local wines, especially in Valladolid. Many of them are good, and some of them have a considerable reputation. Your best guide will be your waiter.

Sherry deserves separate mention: You'll probably find that you will stick to the light, or *fino,* sort. The familiar names of Williams and Humbert, Gordon, Sandemann, and so on are not very often met in Spain, they being almost exclusively export houses. The "cellars"— although sherry is aged entirely above ground—best known to the Spaniard are: *Casa González, Byass,* whose excellent finos are "Tío Pepe" (the lightest of all sherries), and "Viña AB"; *Casa Pedro Domecq,* for its "Fino la Ina"; *Casa Osborne,* for its "Fino la Quinta"; *Casa Garvey* for its "San Patricio"; and *Terry* for its "Cambrio"; *Casa Bobadilla;* and Zoilo make up a useful list.

You should also be reminded that sherries test out at 20 to 22 per cent of alcohol by *weight,* this being about 45 proof. If pressed too closely, sherry can bite the hand that feeds it.

As for sherry's cousin, *manzanilla,* the two most respected labels are "Manzanilla la Guita" and "Manzanilla la Gitana." Distinctly lighter than sherry, it is splendid chilled.

Water. Tap water is suitable for drinking in most areas, although in some places it is over-chlorinated. Madrid tap water is excellent, and is often served at the table and called simply *"agua de Madrid."* Spanish mineral waters are excellent. They are bottled either plain, without gas *(sin gas),* or sparkling with gas *(con gas),* and are ordered accordingly. Among the best brands are Vichy-Catalán and Lanjarón from the mountain springs in the Province of Granada.

LOS TOROS

For the visitor to Spain, bullfighting is the first and most characteristic spectacle of the Peninsula. If you hope to develop even a shadow of the Spaniard's appreciation of the art, you have much reading and watching to do. But even if you do not expect to become an *aficionado,* you can at least learn why loud protests from us about "the poor horses" or "the poor bulls" make little sense to the Spaniard. And you can learn enough to honestly enjoy the *fiesta brava.*

The *toro bravo,* the fighting bull, is not a dairy cow. For centuries famous families of breeders have been creating this savage, deadly animal. He is out to kill anything that moves. And a great *matador* or *torero* will dare him to do just that.

If it is expertly done, the display of bravery, skill, power, and grace in a bullfight will wring you dry of emotion and strength. The skillful matador accomplishes the shattering effect of a ballet dancer on a sword blade on the edge of a precipice.

Once he becomes a ranking maestro, the odds against the torero are unattractive. The average life of the active matador has been set at eight years. Why does he take up the profession? An inner satisfaction, the fame that for one of his position can only come from fighting the bulls, an inner compulsion to create this strange art out of danger—and the

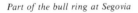

Part of the bull ring at Segovia

The great Ordoñez in the Toledo ring

money involved. Today's ranking matadors, Jose Marí Manzanares, Julio Robles, Niño de la Capea, and Espartaco, are said to rake in tens of thousands of dollars for an afternoon's *corrida* in Madrid.

Assume that you have told the concierge to buy you a brace of *sombra* tickets (seats on the shady side). Here are the characters you are about to watch.

The bull: Five-year-olds, extremely dangerous, were once used, but you will see three-year-olds—not safe, but safer. For one thing, their horns are not as long. You will see that hump of muscles at the bull's neck lift a horse and rider off the ground—and a torero or two, likely enough.

The horse: Protected somewhat, but still an unpleasant necessity in the drama. The best that can be said about him is that if he were not here, he would be in the glue factory.

The men include: The *monosabios,* "handy Andys" who do odd jobs in and about the arena; including hauling out bull corpses; the *picador,* riding the nag mentioned before, who meets the charge of the bull with a stopped lance; and the *banderilleros,* who handle the cape in the first act and who, when the matador elects, plant the *banderillas,* twenty-eight-inch barbed darts, in the bull's withers.

The *presidente,* usually some town official with an expert adviser or two, who directs the progress of the fight through its various scenes, and at the end decides whether the matador shall receive the honor of ears and tail.

The bullfight is held in the *plaza de toros,* sometimes the village square, sometimes a huge bull ring with twenty thousand seats, and usually on a summer Sunday afternoon and especially on local fiesta days.

The drama itself can be classically divided into three acts each five to seven minutes long.

Act One. A trumpet sounds. The gate opens, and the bull emerges at furious speed, looking for someone on whom to vent his purebred rage. The matador must learn quickly the individual characteristics of his bull, since he will live intimately with the points of those slashing horns for deadly and beautiful minutes. The banderilleros drag their capes in front of the bull, so that the matador can see how he hooks and charges.

Then the matador steps out on the sand. At this moment the test of greatness begins. The bull is compelled to charge furiously, to waste his tremendous energies, and to toss his great head wildly enough to begin to soften that huge crest of muscles in his hump. The matador's art lies in imposing this compulsion with the maximum risk to himself, fused with the maximum grace of hand, foot, and body. This he does with the cape, into which the bull lunges headlong, infuriated at its elusiveness. The various "passes" with the cape are beyond identification by the uninitiated, but they are all based upon the *pase verónica,* which leads into the *media verónica* and finally into the whirling circular grace of the *rebolera,* in which the cape swings out like the flying skirt of a dancer.

Three things determine the quality of the matador: the shape, flow, and rhythm of his cape; the posture of his body—he stands erect and must not shift his feet during certain *passes;* and how close he works to the plunging bull. With a great *maestro,* you will hear the bull brush the sequins on the famous "suit of lights."

The picador wields an eight-foot *pica;* the horse takes a mauling. And on occasion so does his low-caste rider. Three times the bull rams his twelve hundred pounds into the horse and each time receives the pike in his shoulder. And three times the matadors, in the order of the day's ranking, perform the *quite,* luring the furious beast away with their capes.

Act Two. The trumpet sounds again, and two or three pairs of banderillas are planted in the bull's withers, either by the banderilleros or, if he has a gift that way, by the matador himself.

Act Three. With the sound of the trumpet the final act, the reason and prepared conclusion for all this, opens. In the hands of a true maestro it mounts to an unbelievable crescendo.

After the matador has received permission to kill the bull from the president and has dedicated it to some one of the spectators—or to them all—the great moments begin. He thrusts his sword into the fold of a small red cloth, the *muleta,* secured to a wooden stick. Grasping sword and stick in his right hand, he puts the bull through the supreme test of the dangerous muleta passes. Since the muleta is small, bull and man are almost one, body to body as the man winds the bull around him in the punishing, wrenching passes, dominates him, controls his movements to a deadly inch, and brings him at last to the point of standing still. Here the matador may improvise and invent, standing with feet apart, with feet together, kneeling, or even—if he has really dominated his bull—backing away on his knees and compelling the bull to follow him.

Finally the matador plants his bull with its front feet together and

One of the Basque forms of pelota or Jai Alai

makes him lower his head so that the downward curving blade of his sword may find the chink between the shoulder blades and sever the aorta near the heart. Then he raises his blade, sights along it, and leaps forward. To reach that spot, he must leap between the deadly horns, and then leap out and away to the left over the right horn. If the muleta is properly used, the sword can be properly used. If it is not, the sword cannot be—and the matador will very likely be tossed or gored. But in this great "moment of truth" that you are watching, the sword gets home to the hilt, and the slight figure incredibly clears the horns. The bull stands motionless for a second or two, then abruptly drops upon the sand. If the matador has pleased the crowd, it will demand an ear —or two ears, the tail—from the presidente as an honor for him.

This, admittedly, is bullfighting at its best. It is not always that. It can be—and often is—brutally gory. But if you have the luck to see a master at the top of his form, you will have experienced drama of an intensity you never dreamed possible.

PARTICIPATION SPORTS

It is unlikely that you will want to spend much of your limited time in sports activities, and if you do, you probably know what the facilities are like.

Golf is booming in Spain, where you can play year-round, generally on new courses. Since the fairways are dry, you get an enormous run on every stroke. Many resort hotels and villa complexes are built around Robert Trent Jones 18-hole courses. The Costa del Sol has so many golf clubs and championship courses that it is often nicknamed "The Costa del Golf." If you're really interested, write to the National Tourist Office of Spain and request the brochure, *Golf in Spain.*

Fishing and hunting are both to be had. There is some big game, and birds such as quail and the European partridge are found in fair quantity. Duck in season. Brown trout up to eight or ten pounds have been taken from the mountain lakes and there is excellent salmon fishing in the rivers of Galicia.

Opportunities for rock- and mountain-climbing are, of course, unlimited in Spain, and there are many devoted groups of *alpinistas* (mountain climbers). There is some skiing in the mountains near Madrid, but the best is to be found in the Catalán and Aragonese Pyrenees.

PELOTA

Pelota, which the Basques, its inventors and rabid devotees, call *Jai Alai,* stands next to the bullfight as a Spanish spectacle.

It is played in a great hall called the *frontón,* and follows the general plan of handball. The version played with the arm-long basket scoop called the *chistera* is formidable in its pace and excitement. The ball, caught on the rebound or at the volley, is played against the far end wall with rifle-shot speed—at such velocity, in fact, that players have been killed by it.

Every bit as fast, and much more frantic to the uninformed traveler, is the betting. The instant the game begins, bookies are on their feet in front of the spectators' seats shouting odds on the play, changing them every few seconds until the match reveals which way it's going. With absolutely incomprehensible signs, the spectators place their bets, and the ear-splitting uproar brays along, mounting to a frenzy when the players are well matched.

THE PASEO

For uncounted centuries the evening *paseo* in Spanish towns has been the focus of the community life. From six to seven in the evening, the fathers and mothers, the young men and the girls, and the little children walk.

In whatever Spanish town you may be, as the hour approaches try to get a table alongside the paseo. (In Seville it's the famous Sierpes; in Madrid, the great boulevard of the Castellana, and lesser streets for more remote *barrios* of the city.) Generally, no wheeled traffic will appear and the crowd will flow like a noisy cataract through the artificial gorge of buildings, which reflect and multiply the noise. At six the raw elements of the community parade are on hand: young men, civilian and military, are already on patrol; girls drift in with female friends or with relatives at either end of the long parade. At first the pace of the girls is brisk, but when the hour strikes they will check this nonfunctional speed to a more useful, calculated stroll, ready to smile or bow if the parents or relatives with them are beginning to think well of the young man. By the sound alone you will be able to tell the moment when the walking becomes official and approved.

SOME QUICK FACTS

Newspapers and Magazines. In the larger cities, and practically every tourist destination, U.S., English and international papers and magazines are on the stands—either the *International Herald Tribune,* and the *Daily Mail,* or air-mail editions flown in from London. Elsewhere you will fall back on the Spanish press. Censorship, once tight, has completely relaxed as part of the trend toward liberalization and democratic procedures. Magazines follow the flag, too. In the larger cities you can pick up *Newsweek* and *Time,* their British, French, German, and Italian counterparts, and a wide selection of other U.S. and English-language publications.

Mail. Spanish post offices are as a rule splendidly concealed and formidably intricate in their operations.

If you will remember that a Spaniard's surname is double and that he is called by the first one, his father's surname, you will avoid certain difficulties when asking for your mail. Your name, say, is W. Frederick Jones. The Spaniard is likely to assume that you are called "Mr. Frederick" (paternal), rather than "Mr. Jones" (maternal). And after a glance at your passport, he is likely to look for your mail under "F," not "J." Have him look under both.

Shipping Packages. Bulky, heavy purchases or personal effects that are no longer needed are best shipped home. The American Express Company provides such a service. Their Madrid main office is located at Plaza de las Cortes, 2 (429-57-75).

Telephone. If you know some Castilian or are merely familiar with Spanish ordinal numerals, you will not find local calls difficult. The operators are extremely courteous and helpful. But don't group your figures. Recite them number by number: 37 05 62 is *"tres siete cero cinco seis dos,"* not *"treinta y siete cero cinco sesenta y dos."* You will need a slug, a *ficha,* for public phones found in bars and restaurants. Street phones operate with a five peseta piece.

Most long distance calls in Spain, at least between the larger cities, can now be accomplished by direct dialing.

For some mysterious reason, the person calling always uses the word *"Oiga"*—"Listen"—instead of "Hello." And the person called invariably uses *"Diga"*—"Speak"—for *his* "Hello." You therefore will answer your telephone calls with the opening gambit of *"Diga."*

Tobacco. At most hotels you can usually find American cigarettes, and street vendors usually have a supply. In metropolitan centers, you will

Boats of the Yacht Club at San Sebastián

find American brands at the Tobacco Monopoly shops, where you may also buy stamps. The price is usually around 250 pesetas.

Cloth and Clothing. Spanish woolen goods are a bit harsher than English, but they wear well and come in a great variety of patterns. The top Spanish tailors in Madrid and Barcelona are very good, and the cost of a well-made, well-cut suit, with three fittings before the final stitching in the English manner, will run about $300, an excellently tailored overcoat, the same. See the shopping notes in the *Fact Finder* section of this guide or ask at the National Tourist Office for addresses.

Electricity. Spain's hydroelectric system has much improved, and the once common electrical failures and dim lighting are no longer a problem.

220 volt 50 cycle AC current is today the most prevalent in Spain, though 110 volt current still exists. Check on exactly what current you have before you plug anything in. You will have no trouble finding a plug converter to fit the outlets in Spain.

Pets. There is no quarantine in Spain. A certificate of good health and proper shots, signed by a veterinarian and certified by the Spanish Consulate is required. Pet food is available.

Fiestas and Ferias. Any time, almost anywhere in Spain a village, town, or city will be *en fiesta* or *en feria,* during which time nothing much moves except the spirits of the people. This is one reason for inquiring ahead as you make your tour. Another equally persuasive reason is the very special charm and atmosphere of the Spanish fiesta and feria, the former having to do with saints, the latter chiefly with animals.

The most important *ferias* are:
In Madrid, la "San Isidro." May 15th with the most important bullfights of all the season.
In Sevilla: "Feria De Sevilla." One week after Easter.
In the Province of Huelva: "NUESTRA SEÑORA DEL ROCIO" First few days of June.
In Pamplona: Fiesta de Pamplona 7th of July
In Valencia: Fiesta de Valencia "Las Fallas," the 19th of March.
In Zaragoza: Fiesta "Del Pilar." The 12th of October.
Over Easter Holy Week. It is well worth watching the villages' processions especially in old towns like Toledo, Granada, Córdoba and Sevilla.

The National Tourist Office of Spain will be able to supply you with a calendar of most of these occasions. Since many of them are movable dates, be sure that the calendar you have is current.

THE ARTS OF SPAIN—IN A WORD

Spain is rich with centuries of art—extraordinary accomplishments in architecture, painting, music, and dancing. Here is a scandalously

Flamenco dancer at Granada

brief mention of the art treasures that for some people will certainly be the climax of their trip.

Music. What most of us think of as "Spanish" music is Andalusian—raw, turbulent, emotional and ancient. It came from Greece, Persia and Byzantium by way of the invading Arabs. It runs heavily to the minor and it is commonly a complex, ornamented music that only the virtuoso guitarist and the trained singer handle gracefully.

Basically there are two kinds of Spanish singing: the *Cante Jondo*—deep, somber and grave; and the *Cante Flamenco,* a gayer and more animated type. Flamenco, the great Spanish dance music, includes many local forms: the *granadinas,* the *malagueñas,* the *alegrías* and the *bulerías*—all named for their places of origin. Andalucía has much flamenco, but if you want the authentic article, you will have to be steered to the right spots by a knowledgeable native.

Dancing. The fame of Spanish dancing goes back to ancient times. Some 3,000 girls from Cádiz—the most famous dancing girls of antiquity—were at one time offering their spectacularly torrid wares in Rome.

It is the *flamenco* dancing of the south that you identify as Spanish, and Andalucía is the place to see it at its best. The shows at the *tablaos* (flamenco nightclubs) in Madrid and Barcelona are primarily for foreigners. The dancers develop unbelievable speed and finesse in the traditional movements—the *meneo,* the whirling turn; the *zapateado,* the stamping; the *taconeo,* the castanet-like heel tapping; the *cimbrado,* the swaying bend of the body. The *fandango* and *sevillanas* are popular everywhere. *Sevillanas* has even found its way into Madrid's discos and is the new dance. In the *seguidilla,* it is said, you must "dance sitting

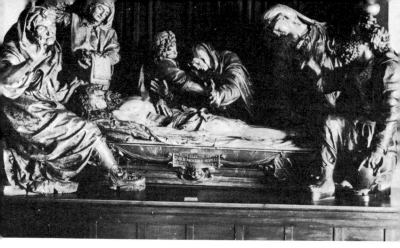

Burial of Christ, *woodcarving by de Juni, San Gregorio*

down"—a perfect description of the steady, motionless body and shoulders above the busy hips, legs, and feet. The *vito,* a specialty of Cádiz, is usually danced by one woman—preferably on a table-top set with brimming wine glasses.

Architecture. The history of Spain is tangible in its architecture—*castros* (fortified towns) and *dolmens* (burial places) from pre-history; Greek remains along the southern coast; and impressive evidences of the Roman centuries in the bridges, roads, aqueducts, walls and cities throughout the country. The middle centuries live as nowhere else in Europe in the cathedrals and castles in Spain. Pre-Romanesque monuments of the 8th, 9th and 10th centuries such as Sta. Maria del Naranco and San Miguel de Lillo, both in Oviedo, have special interest and originality. Romanesque, dominant from the 10th to the 14th century, is best represented in the soaring Cathedral of *Santiago de Compostela,* the Gothic by those at León, Burgos, Seville Oviedo, Segovia and Toledo. They were followed by the uniquely Spanish style called *plateresco,* because of the intricate carving which ornamented it, and a variation, *Isabeline,* which was Gothic in structure but plateresque in ornament. The most distinctive Spanish style was the Moorish—called *mozárabe* when done by Christians under Arab rule and *mudéjar* when done by Moors under Christian domination. Expert artisans and architects, the latter built the hundreds of mudéjar churches you will see in Spain. Their art is characterized by patterned brick work, ceramic decoration, and lavish ornamentation with geometric designs worked in small pieces of wood or intricately carved in plaster. In the beginning of this century the world famous architect Antonio Gaudi designed several outstanding buildings in the *modernista* style. Among them: The *Sagrada Familia* church, el *Parque Guëll* and other masterpieces in Barcelona.

Painting. Spanish painting matured as early as the 14th century, but it flared to impressive heights in what the Spanish call the *Siglo de Oro,* the Golden Age, from about 1550 to 1700. Early masters—Ribalta, Ruelas, Moro, and Coello—were followed by some of the great painters of all times:

Domenico Theotocopuli, called *El Greco* (1548–1625), was born in Crete of Spanish refugees from Córdoba. Much of his finest work is in the Prado, but one of his great paintings, *The Martyrdom of St. Maurice,* hangs in the Escorial, and his finest, *The Burial of the Conde de Orgaz,* is in Santo Tomé in Toledo. He lived and did most of his work in Toledo.

Velásquez (1599–1660) did his great court paintings in Madrid, and developed his style in Italy. He is thought by many to be the greatest technician who ever lived. In many ways, he was a pioneer of Impressionism and modern painting. See him in the Prado. (Page 56.)

Murillo (1618–1682) worked with Velásquez in Madrid, and many of his best paintings are in the Prado. Other fine examples are in the *Hermandad de la Caridad* in Seville.

Goya (1746–1828), next to Velásquez Spain's greatest painter, followed the Golden Age and seemed untouched by it. He worked with a strength and fury almost unequalled in the history of art. The whole range of his work, from his savage satirical paintings of the royal family to his colorful tapestry designs, is in the Prado.

Polychrome Wood Sculpture. Developed by the Spanish during the 16th and 17th centuries, this unique art relied for its effect on two elements—an incredible skill in the craft of realistic carving, and the ability (and willingness) to capture agonizing emotion at its peak. The sculptures in this style are fantastically real—the blood of the Crucifixion oozes almost visibly, the scars are carved and painted with a remarkable taste for torture, tears are forever preserved in glistening glass beads. The most complete collection is in the museum of San Gregorio in Valladolid.

Ceramics and Ironwork. Spanish glazed and colored tile and ware is as old as Roman Spain. It ended in the 17th century with the expulsion from Spain of the Moors, the most expert practitioners of the craft, and the exhaustion of the clay beds. A little second-rate ware is still to be bought; the best is all in museums.

The Spanish also excel in the creation of decorative wrought work, from delicate little window grills to massive forty-foot screens in the cathedrals at León, Toledo and Seville. The *rejas,* as they are called, are everywhere. You can even buy small domestic items in the Rastro, the Flea Market of Madrid.

MADRID

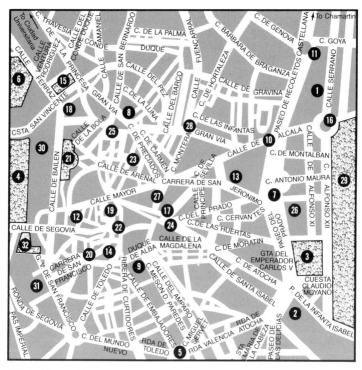

Principal thoroughfares only.

Points of Interest

1) Archeological Museum
2) Atocha Station
3) Botanical Gardens
4) Campo Del Moro
5) GTA De Embajadores
6) Parque Del Oeste
7) Plaza Canovas Del Castillo
8) Plaza Del Callao
9) Plaza De Cascorro
10) Plaza De Cibeles
11) Plaza De Colon
12) Plaza Del Cordon
13) Plaza De Las Cortes
14) Plaza De La Debada
15) Plaza De España
16) Plaza De La Independencia
17) Plaza De Jacinto Benavente
18) Plaza De La Marina Espanola
19) Plaza Mayor
20) Plaza De Moros
21) Plaza De Oriente
22) Plaza De Puerta Cerrada
23) Plaza San Martin
24) Plaza De Santa Ana
25) Plaza De Santo Domingo
26) Prado Museum
27) Puerta del Sol
28) Red De San Luis
29) Retiro Park
30) Royal Palace
31) San Francisco El Grande
32) Vistillas Park

CHAPTER 4

MADRID

You expect to find the essence of a country in its capital. To the visitor, London is England, and Paris is France. But Madrid, you will see, is not Spain; in many ways it is scarcely Spanish at all. Spain is ancient, but Madrid is comparatively young.

The capital does have its ancient history. It is mentioned in 921, when the Asturian king, Ramiro II, took it briefly from the Caliphate. The Moors themselves built a large fortress here, as a foreguard of Toledo, only fifty miles away to the south. Isabella and Ferdinand held court here several times. And Philip II formally established the village of Madrid as his capital in 1561. But aside from a few houses around the *Casa de la Villa* and several churches of the 17th century, very little of this history shows.

If you don't expect Madrid to be Spain, you are properly prepared to enjoy it. Capital life is vibrant and full of energetic currents; it is animated, made so by one of the most talkative people on earth. Madrid loves to go to dinner—at 10:30, don't forget—and to theaters and *verbenas* and *paseos;* and the city, stretching along either side of the long boulevard of the Castellana, is wonderfully bright and spacious.

You should make Madrid the hub of the wheel of your visit to Spain, branch out along the spokes, and then return to rest in Madrid's metropolitan comfort and convenience. Prepare to dine late and break-fast late. Visit your few churches and museums in the morning, since most of them will be shut in the afternoon; lunch, but lightly; stay out of the hot clear sun until four. Stroll along the Gran Via from four to six; shift then, as well-dressed Madrid does, to the Castellana and there stroll, or sit and take coffee while you watch the cheerful, talkative, well-mannered world go by. Or go to the quarter crossed by the Calle

The Alcala Gate leads into central Madrid

de la Cruz (near the Puerta del Sol) or to the Calle de Cuchilleros (near the Plaza Mayor) where there are hundreds of small bars.

Coming in from the airport at Barajas, you enter Madrid through a great canyon of new apartment houses. The street empties into the beautiful Castellana, and you pass several monuments in their traffic circles, called *glorietas.* Then the wide, long, green sweep of the boulevard brings you grandly down the double rank of trees to the circular *Plaza de Cibeles,* with the Mother-goddess herself seated in her lion-drawn chariot in the middle of a fountain. The phantasm of architecture to your left there is the general post office—the *Palacio de Comunicaciones* which, because of its cathedral-like grandeur, is nicknamed *"Nuestra Señora de las Comunicaciones."*

Here the "old" city begins. To your left the Calle de Alcalá brings you past the famous park of the *Retiro.* To the right the Gran Via runs down into the big Plaza de España; Calle Alcalá itself continues through shops and cafés, hatteries, booteries and bookshops until it spills out into the huge square of the Puerta del Sol—Sun Gate—and on down the Arenal to the Royal Palace. If you include the Paseo del Prado, the prolongation of the Castellana down to the Mediodía railway station, you have here the limits within which the tourist will "see" the city.

The "Old Madrid" of the Hapsburg kings has its own 17th-century atmosphere. Madrid was once referred to as a "villa" (town), hence the name of its town square, Plaza de la Villa, enclosed by the plateresque palace, Casa Cisneros. Its 17th-century town hall, Casa de la Villa, was designed by Juan Gómez de Mora. The adjacent medieval house and tower of the Lujanes family dates to the 15th century, before Madrid was even founded.

Along one long side of Madrid's main square, the Plaza Mayor, built between 1617 and 1619, are balconies from which nobility and royalty would watch the important events of the day—bullfights, burning of heretics, canonization of saints, and circuses. In the center, the great bronze equestrian statue of King Philpe III, who ordered construction of the Plaza, faces east toward the Castellana and the Prado Museum, which belong to yet another Madrid, the Madrid of the Bourbon dynasty of kings.

The Bourbon monarchs, in a great spate of building in the 18th century, gave Madrid another aspect of its present character. Philip V, the first of these, sought to brighten up the place and give it importance. In 1726, the Palace and gardens of the Retiro were built for his residence, and in 1734, when the old palace was burned from under him, he began the huge Royal Palace.

Charles III gave the capital its spacious bright quality, with the help of two first-rate architects, Ventura Rodríguez and Juan de Villanueva. Long before the Champs Elysées was laid out by Baron Haussmann to delight the Parisians, the strollers of Madrid were thronging the green shade and the immense width of the Castellana.

For the sight-seer, Madrid is not difficult. If you are very short of time, you can come away with a worthwhile recollection of Spain's capital by visiting three places: **the Prado Museum; the Retiro Park; the Plaza Mayor.**

The 17th-century City Hall of Madrid, Casa de la Villa

If you can spend an additional day or so—without skimping the rest of Spain—you will want to add to them: the **Royal Palace and Armory;** the *Goya frescoes* in the dome of the **Ermita de San Antonio de la Florida;** the **Rastro;** the church of **San Francisco el Grande;** the **Ciudad Universitaria,** the University.

THE PRADO

No sensible way of seeing a great museum has yet been devised, and the Prado is one of the three or four truly great museums of the world. It is long and high, and it contains more than 3,000 paintings, most of them of high quality. If you have ample time, there are few buildings in the world in which it can be better spent. If your stay in Madrid is limited, however, you will probably do best to concentrate on the three greatest of the several great Spanish masters, Velásquez, Goya, and El Greco, plus, if you're in fighting trim, Rubens and the great northern European collection of paintings by Hieronymus Bosch, Roger van der Weyden, Brueghel the Elder, Tiziano, Frangélica, Rafaël and Dürer, almost every one a masterpiece of the first rank.

One of the oldest collections in Europe, the Prado was begun by Charles I and enhanced by Philip II and Philip IV. Philip V added the

The Titian Room of the Prado

Madrid's Congreso de los Diputados

important French section, and even the deplorable Ferdinand VII did his part by combining at the Prado all the royal art of the various palaces. Finally, in 1840, the early Spanish and Flemish paintings taken from the monasteries were added. Because hundreds of great paintings are concentrated here in clearly defined and grouped schools, the impact is stunning, not diffuse; it is single and solid, like being struck by a club instead of a broom.

Designed in the neo-classic style by the Spanish architect, Juan de Villanueva, the two-story building was constructed over a period of some thirty years, starting in 1785. Some additions were made later on in the 19th century. Originally, it was intended to be a museum of natural history, but Ferdinand VII, at the instigation of his wife, María Isabel de Braganza, decided to put it to its present use and, when the building was inaugurated in 1819, it contained only Spanish paintings. Eventually, the collection became so large that in 1894, the contemporary paintings were moved to a separate museum called the *Casón del Buen Retiro,* where Picasso's dramatic *Guernica* is now displayed.

Even for an hour's visit, a guidebook will be useful. If nothing else, it will help you locate the high points you wish to take in. (There is an excellent one in English available at the entrance.) With its help, you can find your way to the El Greco rooms. Three of the greatest El Grecos (the *San Mauricio* of the Escorial, the *Conde Orgaz* of Toledo, and the *View of Toledo* of the Metropolitan Museum in New York) are missing, but the collection remains an astonishing one. It includes the extraordinary portrait, *El Caballero de la Mano en el Pecho.*

In addition to the Casón del Buen Retiro, which is actually two separate museums on different levels of the building, the Prado has also overflowed into the Villahermosa Place, which has lovely gardens as well as 215,000 square feet of exhibit space. The palace is located diagonally across the Plaza Cánovas del Castillo, the tree-lined traffic circle dominated by the adored Neptune Fountain. One 400-peseta ticket, obtainable at either entrance, will admit you to all four galleries.

The Velásquez collection is dominated by *Las Hilanderas* (The Spinners), where light and more light dazzles through the colors as though the morning sun were shining through the wall behind the canvas. There are the other famous pictures: Philip IV as a huntsman, faithfully and pathetically and greatly painted; the little Don Baltasar Carlos on his little Flemish horse; the equestrian portrait of the Condeduque; and the buffoon-dwarfs, painted with a tenderness that is as extraordinary as is the reality. Finally, the Surrender of Breda *(Las Lanzas),* where Velásquez inserted a self-portrait at the right. If you abruptly find yourself estimating the tonnage of the *Three Graces* so sumptuously painted by Rubens—sixty of whose pictures hang in the Prado—you will know that you have gone too far.

You can also see one of the great paintings of the West, Velásquez' *Las Meninas* (The Maids of Honor). The central figure is the little princess Margarita María. To her right kneels one of the maids of honor, Doña María Agustina Sarmiento, while another, Doña Isabel Velasco, stands immediately to the princess' left hand. Farther right, in the foreground, is another demonstration of the artist's fusion of sympathy with reality: the two dwarf-buffoons of Margarita María, "Little Nicky" Pertusato, and the head-heavy Mari Barbola. Another *dama de honor,* Doña Marcela de Ulloa, stands in the middle distance

The Velasquez Room of the Prado

to the right, with a palace servitor, and the Queen's major-domo, Don Juan Nieto, is framed by the doorway in the background. Velásquez painted himself as at work on a portrait of Philip IV and his wife, Mariana, whose faces appear in the mirror above the princess' head. To say that technically this painting is an extraordinary achievement is to make an understatement.

The almost incredible range of Goya's artistic vision is fully represented in the Prado. Here is the royal family of Charles IV—the painting is fairly livid with savage indignation. Here also are the two *Majas,* a *maja* in general being a colorful *madrileña* (lady of Madrid) of a certain reputation. She is nude *(desnuda)* in one of the paintings and clothed *(vestida)* in the other, and is still labeled by legend the Duchess of Alba. (The story is that the duke got wind of the *Maja Desnuda* one night and appeared next morning armed with all the weapons required by the occasion; and that Goya, hearing of the duke's intention, had stayed up all night painting the *Maja Vestida* to show how innocent the whole affair had been.)

In the process of seeking out these three great Spanish masters, you will perhaps have a moment to pause before Ribera's great *El Martiro de San Bartolome* the beautiful *San Mateo* of Ribalta, the *Martyrdom of St. Bartholomew,* or a Zurburan still life. With limited time you will probably not want to look at more than a few of the more than sixty paintings by Rubens before going on to the rest of the great Flemish collection. Elsewhere, of course, there are works by Fra Angélico, Veronese, Tintoretto and many others—in short, the Prado is a museum worthy of arranging your travel schedule around, so as to make sure that your time there is not limited.

The Retiro and the monument to Alfonso XII

THE RETIRO

The Retiro Gardens were planned for Philip II as the forest park attached to a Norman castle in which his queen, the English Mary Tudor, was to live. But Mary never had the opportunity of occupying the castle, and in 1631 it was turned into the Royal Palace of the *Buen Retiro,* of which nothing now remains but the Salón de Reinos building which now houses the fascinating *Museo del Ejercito,* the Military Museum that recalls the memories of Spain's glorious defeats and the *Casa del Buen Retiro,* an annex of the Prado Museum. From then until the reign of Charles III, the Retiro was the residence of the kings for most of the year. In 1869, the Retiro was turned over to the municipal authorities as the Public Park of Madrid.

The Retiro is more trees than grass and flowers, but the trees are splendid; and never, even in the bitterest droughts, have they gone without water. This is not a senseless extravagance in an arid land, for the Retiro is the last remnant of the great forest that once surrounded Madrid. For generations these trees have been preserved. A century and a half ago, during the War of Independence, the French and the English both constructed fortifications in the Retiro. But neither of them cut down the forest of Madrid, nor did the Republicans, during the three-year Franquist siege.

Here, in the intense dry heat of summer, are three hundred and fifty acres of shade in the heart of Madrid. Here, too, are dozens of fountains and a large artificial lake, the *Estanque*—dominated by a massive columned monument topped by an equestrian statue of King Alfonso XII. You can paddle a canoe around the lake, or sit in the shade at an outdoor café watching the people enjoying themselves.

There is plenty of exploring to do in the Retiro. You can't miss the magnificent Crystal Palace which is used for exhibitions, but you might have a hard time finding the statue of the Fallen Angel. The park is never locked at night, and no crime seems to go on there. The principal nocturnal activity here is at the Florida Park nightclub housed in an old converted stable called *Casa de Vacas.*

For many visitors the memorable thing about this tag end of forest is that there are birds here. Spain is a bird watcher's paradise but also a hunter's paradise. The former will find not only all sorts of migrating birds but also song birds, and the latter can shoot partridge, quail, and turtle doves in the nearby mountains.

THE RASTRO

The Rastro seems to be nothing more than an enormous "Flea Market," acres of the most astounding assortment of junk—until you discover the little patio where the shops are located. In these, you will find objects quite as astonishing and much more interesting than those spread out along the street. Rare and beautiful things are forever being discovered here, but they are not necessarily cheap. But with a keen eye, you can find treasures among the junk of the street vendors. They often may have valuable antiques and even museum pieces, without having any idea of their value. Many buy out old attics and try to unload the lot at the Rastro. This is the place for *regateo,* or bargaining —never pay the asking price. Everything that goes on at the Rastro happens on Sunday morning, and the earlier you get there the better.

THE PALACIO REAL

What can be said of this grandiose Royal Palace? Begun in 1738, first lived in years later by Charles III, one hundred and sixty feet high, four hundred and seventy feet square, with some thirty enormous principal *salones,* red-velvet tapestried walls, Tiepolo and Mengs ceilings, twenty-five hundred large Spanish and Flemish tapestries, the Royal Library with its nineteen rooms and more than one hundred thousand volumes, an entirely fascinating Royal Pharmacy—here, indeed, is a royal palace. Also, the fact that its furnishings are in place distinguishes it from other European palaces, and this one is a must.

Interior of the Royal Palace

One display should not be skipped: the *Real Armeria* (the Royal Armory), the most complete collection of medieval arms and armor in the world. Charles I, who established it, left his armor to the museum. In the vestibule you will see the armor of Philip II, and that of his queen, Mary Tudor. The steel cuirass of the notable pirate Barbarossa is there, as are the swords of Isabella's Ferdinand, of Francisco Pizarro, the conqueror of Peru and Hernán Cortés, conqueror of Mexico.

Two things will surprise you: the extremely rich and skillful craftsmanship of the armor and swords, and the astonishingly small size of the men who wore these suits on their way to the conquest of a vast empire. When you handle the two-handed sword of one of Spain's great soldiers and captains, Don Juan of Austria, you will find it almost impossible to squeeze both your hands into the two-handed grip. It can be wielded easily with one hand.

ERMITA DE SAN ANTONIO DE LA FLORIDA

Goya painted his extraordinary and quite unecclesiastic frescoes in the dome of the Ermita shortly after it was completed in 1798. His view of saints and angels was much the same as Zurbarán's at Guadalupe. These holy people above your head were taken fresh from the streets of Madrid. The female personages in particular seem rather to belong to other "abbeys" than those appointed in Heaven. Required seeing, but not until you have been to the Prado.

SAN FRANCISCO EL GRANDE

The grandest church in Madrid, San Francisco el Grande, was begun in 1761. But one of the two first-rate architects of the time, Ventura

A corner of the Retiro Park

University City in Madrid

Rodríguez, found the plans faulty, and in 1778 redrew them to give the church its present resplendent form. Seen from the outside, the dome is spectacular; its rotunda, from within, is magnificent. It is worth recording that its diameter of thirty-three meters is greater than that of St. Paul's in London.

THE CIUDAD UNIVERSITARIA

Begun by Alfonso XIII in 1928, University City was partially destroyed during the Civil War. The siege lines about the city being the northern walls of the university buildings, Franquist artillery battered them into rubble. Much money has since been spent to replace and expand the University, and physically the buildings, walks and gardens add up to one of the most spectacular university centers of Europe. The sons of the Falange and of the bureaucracy have been given heavy preference, but even this careful selection has not been sufficient to suppress heterodoxy among both faculty and students. The Spaniards are an inextinguishable race.

Be sure to visit *El Museo Español de Arte Contemporaneo* (The Spanish Museum of Contemporary Art) located in University City. You will find wonderful paintings and sculpture. 10 A.M.–6 P.M.; Sunday 10 A.M.–3 P.M. Closed Monday.

There is much pleasure in Madrid. And, obviously, there is much more to see than is presented here. It is a sophisticated and captivating city of over four million animated people—so captivating, indeed, that many visitors are tempted to linger there longer than their time budget permits. Madrid will be immensely enjoyable. But remember that you will return often to the capital from your excursions into the rest of the country. And remember, too, that the Spain that lies all about you is every bit as vivid and exciting as Madrid itself.

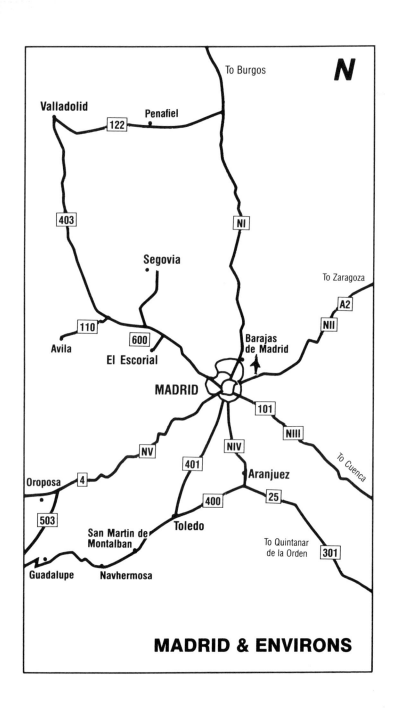

MADRID & ENVIRONS

CHAPTER *5*

WHAT TO SEE IN SPAIN

Spain is a nation of 38,400,000 people and nearly two hundred thousand square miles. You can't see it all in a week, or in a month or in a year. But even if your time is limited, you can see much of it if you use your time properly.

Some of the trips suggested here can be made in a day or two. Many can be cut and combined with others. It is left to you to pick and choose as your time and taste dictate.

AROUND MADRID

You need only a day for the cold, enormous and—if you visit it only once—impressive monastery of the Escorial, the *Royal Monastery of San Lorenzo,* a short hour out of Madrid to the northwest.

Since the trip is short, you will also have time to see the nearby *Valle de los Caídos,* the Valley of the Fallen, a Civil War Memorial. Vastly expensive in money and man hours, it is a great crypt carved and blasted nearly nine hundred feet into the granite of a mountain peak, a tremendous single-aisled, superbly finished cavern, topped by a cross five hundred feet in the air, high above on the peak of the mountain. It is undeniably and overwhelmingly effective.

Philip II built the Escorial as a residence-monastery in the years 1553–1584, an extraordinarily prompt job of building for those days. Mass and proportion are the sole elements that Juan de le Herrera, his architect, had any use for. The monastic church, just inside the main gates, is an illustration. Its dome, rising three hundred feet above the marble floor, rests its weight at the crossing on four enormous piers; and these piers are nearly one hundred and five feet in circumference.

Everything is vast except for the two most impressive sections: the Royal Pantheon, beneath the high altar; and the private apartments of Philip II. His living quarters are generally said to be bare and ascetic. In fact, they rather coincide with our present tastes. You will probably find them quite warm in feeling.

Philip's energetic approach to his faith may be estimated by the massive accumulation of relics in the church: ten entire bodies of saints, one hundred and forty-four heads of saints, three hundred and sixty-six arms and legs, and the thigh of St. Lawrence, displaying the roasted flesh of his martyrdom. This is in keeping with the Escorial, which was built in the shape of a grill!

There are several tours available, depending on your time. But try not to miss the museum in the wing near the living quarters where you can see paintings by El Greco, Velasquez, Ribera, and Hieronymus Bosch.

If the day is warm you will merely be cold as you walk your long round. If it is cold, you will shiveringly wonder how the king and his Jeronymite brethren ever survived. Take a sweater with you. But go you must, for without question this creation of Philip's is one of the world's marvels.

TOLEDO VIA OROPESA AND GUADALUPE

Toledo, 69 kms. south of Madrid, may be visited independently. Or it may be seen as part of the longer trip outlined here.

Oropesa, some 150 kms. southwest of Madrid on the highway Extremadura, has a most impressive castle. You see it on its high platform of rock long before you get to it. And you can spend the night there, for in this grand 15th-century fortress is one of the most striking paradores. Don't miss it. You wind up the crooked, narrow streets of the village, plunge into a long tunnel through the thick wall, and get out of car or bus in the great square of the Plaza de Armas, where the tall donjon keep soars above your head. You then mount the broad staircase, and from the upper balcony enter the huge baronial hall. This is just the lobby of the parador.

The Monastery of Guadalupe. There is no comfortable way of getting to this famous monastery. From **Navalmoral de la Mata** (35 kms. west of Oropesa), over a road of bottomless red dust, you arrive at length at **Talavera la Vieja,** with its important Roman ruins: the graceful columns of a curia, or town hall, the foundations and steps of a large temple, the remains of an aqueduct—and the oldsters of the village sunning themselves on seats made of Corinthian capitals. And for some inexplicable reason, the curate has two El Grecos hanging in his house.

Some 60 kms. southwest of Talavera la Vieja is Guadalupe. The Jeronymite monastery of Santa María, established in the early 15th century, looks like an immense castle rather than a place for monks.

Unimportant until the time of Isabella and Ferdinand, it later acquired enormous prestige. Two facts illustrate this. One is a little jingle of the day:

> Whoever is Count and wants to become Duke
> Had better first become a brother in Guadalupe.

The other is that in 1809 the French invaders hauled away nine carloads of gold and silver from the place.

At Guadalupe you will want to see:

The eight Zurbarán paintings in the *Sacristy.*

The famous *cloister* with its horseshoe-arched arcades.

The *Museo de los Ornamentos,* a magnificent collection of ecclesiastical vestments, woven in the monastery's own shops.

The *Museo de Cantorales,* eighty-nine unique choir books produced by the monastery's 16th-century miniaturists.

The *iron screens,* among the finest in Spain.

Not by any means an old establishment, as these things go in Spain, Guadalupe ended the 17th century with its high walls enclosing an area over ten miles square. It is difficult to conceive the size and complexity of this establishment. Don Juan Pacheco, marqués de Villena, once made a vow to support Guadalupe for a year. After two days his agent sent word that in order to keep his vow he would have to sell all his estates. It took the Pope to get him off the hook.

Simple meals are served to tourists, and quarters are available in the Parador of Guadalupe for the night.

Your return (188 kms.) to Toledo over C401, a poor road through glorious mountains and over the pass, the *puerto de San Vicente,* will not be quick, but it will be rewarding.

Eleven kms. beyond **Navahermosa** and near Toledo, turn left to **San Martín de Montalbán.** One of the fine castles of your entire Spanish experience is near there. Ask the way, for its size and situation above a deep gorge make it tremendously impressive. Most interesting feature: a pointed Gothic arch at least 90 feet high standing alone against the outer walls.

A few kilometers on toward Toledo is the castle of **Guadamur,** on your left. The owners, if not in residence, permit visitors. It is restored with a noble staircase, a truly ducal telephone cabinet in one of the angle towers, and a more than duquesal bathroom occupying another, sunken tub and all. This is a proper Castle in Spain—massive, elegant and credible. Apply to the porter for admission. 10 A.M. to 2 P.M. and 3:30 to 6 P.M. for a small fee.

Toledo. More than two thousand years of civilization—Roman, Visigothic, and Arab—have passed through Toledo. Today it is nearly as it has been for a thousand years. Even the ecclesiastical buildings have merely changed creeds, not sites. The cathedral and many of the lesser churches are in foundation or in structure mosques.

Toledo is not to be described. It has to be seen—and not, except in dire necessity, in one day. Your itinerary should, if possible, include:

The *cathedral,* one of the most impressive of the Peninsula. Enormous, and filled with an unmanageable number of treasures. See it first on your own toward the end of the day, when the lofty aisles are already dark and the sun is shining copper-red through the polychrome glass of the upper windows. Thereafter you will do best to join a guided party to see the treasures of the interior—the choir, the stalls, the rose windows, the works of art, the fabulous treasury.

The *house of El Greco,* and the nearby *El Greco museum.*

A short distance down the hill from the above, the beautiful synagogue, *El Tránsito.* The walls and ceiling are *mudéjar* at its finest.

San Juan de los Reyes, built for Isabella and Ferdinand, an astonishing example of Plateresque Gothic.

The 10th-century mosque turned church, called *Cristo de la Luz.* A jewel of architecture.

The *Casa de la Mesa,* because of the *mudéjar* work in its superb entry decoration and the *artesonado* ceiling.

The *church of Santo Tomé;* El Greco's greatest painting, *The Burial of Count Orgaz,* properly lighted at last.

The *Hospital de Santa Cruz,* most notable for the entrance and the upper gallery of the principal patio.

Tower of the Cathedral at Toledo   *Church of Cristo de la Luz in Toledo*

The *Palacio de Galiana,* near the railway station. An Arab country palace, built in the year 999.

The *Hospital Tavera,* notable for the famous canvas by Ribera: *Una Mujer Barbuda* (the bearded mother nursing her child). Also some others by El Greco.

The *National Arms Factory.* Toledo steel is no longer what it was, but the display room may hypnotize you, so that you will find yourself coming away with a two-handed sword.

The triangular *plaza mayor* of the town, called the *Zocodover,* where you will return to sit and rest with a *fino.*

You should not miss the view of the city at night. Two vantage points are especially good: "La Virgen del Valle" and the National Parador at the top of the hill where you can find sleeping accommodations.

And when you have long overstayed your time limit, then back the 69 short kilometers to Madrid.

MADRID TO ARANJUEZ

Aranjuez, 47 kms. south of Madrid, must be seen. You can make it easily in a day.

Lying in a loop of the Tajo River, Aranjuez is an oasis in the dry Castilian plateau. Around it the river spreads out in a most un-Spanish way. Isabella once planned to develop it as a water route to the Atlantic, and as late as the end of the 18th century, Charles III planned to sail ships down the Tajo to Lisbon. The inevitable drought blasted his plan, but the terminal works, the *Real Casa de Marinos,* are still there.

Beginning with Charles I, the kings of Spain made Aranjuez into a kind of Versailles. In spring and autumn, especially, it is almost unbelievable. The elms (which Philip II brought in from England) and the sycamores are among the largest trees in Europe. As you stroll the gardens you may even hear nightingales sing. You can also visit the Royal Palace and other buildings in the garden.

MADRID TO CUENCA

From **Aranjuez** southeast on the main road it is only 80 kms. to **Quintanar de la Orden,** a short drive for lunch at the *albergue.* Here you are on the edge of the Don Quixote country, where the people take the Knight of the Doleful Countenance to have been a veritable person. They have made a museum out of the house in nearby **El Toboso** where Cervantes placed Don Quixote's Dulcinea. Similarly, the house in **Argamasilla,** further south, where Cervantes was imprisoned and wrote the first few chapters of his book, and in which he had Don Quixote die, has become part of the real history of the countryside.

By this time you will have learned that "Castles in Spain" is more than a figure of speech in this country. Spain still possesses more than a thousand buildings or ruins of buildings that can be fairly described as castles. Among the finest of them are *Loarre,* the *Alcázar of Segovia, Valencia de Don Juan, Peñafiel, Manzanares el Real, Medellín, Medina del Campo, Coca, Peñiscola, Madrigal de las Atlas Torres,* and *Bellver* in Mallorca.

One of the finest, a lordly and almost perfect mountain of masonry, stands in **Belmonte,** 19 kms. southeast of **Quintanar** and then east a bit. Your map may show the latter road as a good secondary route. That will bring you to one of the rewards of your Spanish journey. Let us hope that it will be after four o'clock in the afternoon, with the sun turning reddish gold. The sky will be intensely blue, and Belmonte castle will be a glowing mass of gold. There you will see what a castle should look like.

Built by Don Juan Pacheco in 1456, it might as well have come down from the morning of the world. After you have walked beneath its enormous, thick walls, and along its sentry walks, and gone up the narrow circular staircases to the tops of the huge towers, and looked down into the dungeon to which no exit exists save the hole forty feet above through which the prisoner was lowered—after all of this, you will feel that you are walking through a fantasy.

To most of us, castles are symbols of romance. Belmonte is the perfect example. Over forty years ago, the former Duke of Alba gave it to one of his young friends as a wedding present. Belmonte makes an entirely acceptable present of that sort.

Alarcón de las Altas Torres, a few kms. southeast, is equally impressive. If Belmonte is magnificent but believable, Alarcón de las Altas Torres, built by Alaric, is a prodigious and unearthly place. Beyond two bulging defense towers on the narrow causeway of rock over which you cross the 800-foot gorge of the Júcar River, the town and castle soar into the sky on a rocky pinnacle—an immense, white ghost of walls and towers and narrow streets. There are people here—this is a town within walls. Even the castle's name is part of the fairy-tale atmosphere: Alarcón of the High Towers.

Cuenca, 47 kms. north on N420 from **Olivares,** is not an anticlimax to this unreal day. On the brink of the high cliff opposite the road are the *Casas Colgadas,* the famous Hanging Houses, glued to the precipice. Along the precipitous narrow street leading to its *plaza mayor,* are houses that have ten and twelve stories; it's that steep. Bridges span the deep ravines that gash the cliff. One of them has a hundred and eighty feet of empty space beneath it.

The 16th-century palace that is now the *posada de San José* is an inn in keeping with this day. It wanders over a dozen levels on the brink of the precipice. Under almost any window there is a sheer drop of five hundred feet to the river with its bright border of poplars.

Do not miss the Museum of Abstract Art and the Hanging Houses *(casas colgadas).* You will find contemporary abstract art from many well-known Spanish painters.

NORTHWEST FROM MADRID

The Alcázar in Segovia

Northwest of Madrid, within a radius of 200 kilometers, are some of the most memorable sights of Spain. Many of them can be visited on one-day excursions from the capital. Or you may choose to follow some version of the more leisurely tour outlined here. Arrange your itinerary to fit your own schedule, but don't miss this part of Spain.

MADRID TO SEGOVIA VIA MANZANARES AND LA GRANJA

North of Madrid 75 kms., along the Santillana Reservoir from which Madrid draws its excellent water, is **Manzanares el Real.**

Manzanares castle, built in the latter part of the 15th century, is basically Plateresque Gothic. The southern wall with its charming gallery is straight out of the troubadours' romances; it has nothing to do with guns and defense. The exterior is gloriously intact, but the interior has been restored.

From Manzanares you turn west to the main road north, climb up the pass of Navacerrada—snow here as late as March and as early as October—and wind sharply down to **La Granja.** Just under the 6,000-foot Pico de Peñalara is the Jeronymite monastery founded by Juan I of Castile in the 14th century and substantially remodeled late in the 15th century.

It is not absolutely required that you admire the interior. But three things are impressive about La Granja: 1, the superb avenue of cypresses by which you approach the gates; 2, the magnificent tapestries upstairs, Flemish and Spanish, including some by Goya; 3, the gardens at the foot of the great slope where a magnificent grove of cedars, cypresses, elms and sycamores provides avenues and crossings for the famous fountains. Without water spouting from them these fountain figures are almost grotesque. But if you can manage to be at La Granja when the water is flowing, especially on July 25, you'll find that the fountains are absolutely superb. **Segovia** is the heart of Old Castile and the symbol of Segovia is its fortress-castle, the *Alcázar.* See it first from the river below. Springing high above the tall trees along the river, it rides the cliff with tremendous majesty. Equaled only by Peñafiel, it is both solid history and a symbol of the great illusions of romance.

The rest of Segovia is almost as impressive. The *Aqueduct* was built of heavy granite blocks during the Roman Empire. In all it is 14 kilometers long, and here you will see a 900-foot, double-tiered section that stands 90 feet high where it crosses a ravine. Until 1906 it carried water to the city—2,000 years after it was built. It is still in functioning shape.

The *city walls,* mostly Roman, are virtually intact, though they are so covered by houses that they are not everywhere visible. Best view is at the *Puerta de San Andrés.*

Romanesque churches. Chief among the fine examples here is the Templar church *Vera Cruz* (1208) below the walls and across the Eresma River. It is twelve-sided, and the inner structure is in two stories. Inside and out, Vera Cruz is a gem. Other churches: *San Juan de los Caballeros,* in part 11th century; *San Esteban,* 13th century, with one of the finest towers in Spain; *San Martín,* nearly the prize of the lot, because of its elaborate two-level exterior gallery.

The Cathedral. Built in 1525, it was the last Gothic church of its kind to go up in Spain. Handsome, tall, beautifully spacious, golden in color, it is called *la Dama de las Catedrales de España,* the Lady of Spanish cathedrals.

El Parral. The main chapel has a tremendous tryptich, carved in a quite unbelievable way. For boldness (or sheer nerve), this formidable piece of sculpture has few equals.

This part of Old Castile fairly teems with notable castles and towns. Only a handful of them can be described here. Among those most emphatically worth seeing are:

Turégano, for its *plaza* and the dramatic castle on the hill above.

Pedraza de la Sierra, because it is the most typical medieval town in Castile with narrow streets winding up the hill past venerable 16th-century houses and through city walls to a wide, colonnaded *plaza mayor.* The massive castle stands majestically on its rock. And in the streets almost nothing moves—except the inevitable children, the *chiquillería,* who can spring out of the crevices of a boulder when a foreigner stops to look. Tremendous atmosphere.

Sepúlveda, which lacks only a castle to match Pedraza.

Coca, with a fine *mudéjar* castle.

From Coca to **Valladolid** is a drive of 65 kms. north.

VALLADOLID AREA

A busy, modern city, **Valladolid** has only a few places of interest for the visitor: the beautiful tower of *La Antigua;* the extraordinary façades of *San Pablo* and *San Gregorio;* and the museum in the latter, with a most complete collection of Spanish wood sculpture.

But within easy driving range of Valladolid are two fine castles.

Peñafiel, 50 kms. east, is dominated by a rocky platform some 600 feet long and only 60 feet wide. On this, riding in the sky like a lean white ship, is the castle of *Peñafiel.*

An 11th-century outer wall, and an inner one of the 13th; thirty

San Pablo in Valladolid; Saint Sebastian, *woodcarving, San Gregorio*

round towers; a single gateway at the top of the steep path from the village; an enormously thick central keep towering a hundred feet; a single entry over a movable wooden ramp leading steeply upward to the door—these are the details. This overwhelming attack on one's credulity is required seeing.

Fuensaldaña, 6 kms. north of Valladolid, among the best of the Spanish castles, is also one of the best preserved.

At **Medina del Campo,** 51 kms. southwest of Valladolid, stands *Castillo de la Mota,* the huge brick edifice where Isabella died. **Madrigal de las Altas Torres,** her birthplace, lies 24 kms. farther south over flat and useless earth. But toward sunset the land catches fire, and the tumbled walls, the towers and spires are as memorable as the name, Madrigal of the High Towers. Many of the towers have fallen, but the 13th-century Moorish walls are perfect in their circle.

Ávila, 50 kms. south, is the home of Spain's greatest mystic poet, San Juan de la Cruz, and of one of the most remarkable women who ever lived, Santa Teresa de Jesús. The Spanish attribute the defeat of the Reformation in good part to Santa Teresa, and they have made a phrase for her city: "Avila, the fortress that threw back the Reformation."

Ávila has no castle and needs none. Its walls are enough. More than a mile and a half in circumference, they have eighty-eight half-round towers and nine city gates. Three thousand men worked nine years at the end of the 11th century to rebuild old fortifications that had been battered for three centuries by Arab and Christian. The work was finished in 1099, and the walls have scarcely been touched since. You will see nothing like those walls anywhere in Europe.

Three other things remain to be seen in Ávila:

The former *Convento de Santa Teresa,* a church built on the site of the house where the saint was born.

The *Cathedral,* begun the year the walls were finished. Its apse projects like a huge bastion beyond the walls.

The *Church of San Vicente,* Ávila's finest. Apart from the magnificence of its nave, the two most noteworthy things about it are the west porch, with its extraordinary sculpture, and the extremely interesting 13th-century sepulcher of San Vicente and his two disciples, Santas Sabina and Cristeta.

The province of Ávila is known as the land of saints and stones. You already know about the saints, Santa Teresa and San Juan de la Cruz. In your 60-kilometer run south on C502 into the Gredos Mountains you will find out about the stones. The granite boulders make a terrifying and exhilarating wilderness as you come over the *Puerto de Menga,* and past **Venta del Obispo.** There you should turn straight west for a night at the *Parador de Gredos,* one of the most magnificently situated inns in Spain. All about it stand the 8,000-foot peaks, steel-bright, their silver and bronze mica glittering in the sun.

From Parador de Gredos south to **Arenas de San Pedro** via the *Puerto del Pico* is a spectacular 30-kilometer Alpine drive with a theatrical view of the floor of the Castilian plateau.

This is the beginning of **La Vera,** a green and fertile ribbon, only sixty miles long and less than ten wide, set down in the center of the burned earth of Castile. Thanks to a freak of the southwest Atlantic winds, this tiny country gets heavy rains. It is an oddity—and still a hidden one.

Farther west, at Cuacos, you can turn north to the 15th-century monastery of **Yuste,** and see its very simple two or three rooms, the terrace and the little garden where the Emperor Charles V spent his last years.

From Yuste you can either return to Madrid, stopping a night at the parador in **Oropesa,** or you can turn west to **Plasencia,** and pick up the western trip described later.

THE EAST: PYRENEES AND THE COAST

Castle tower in Olite, near Pamplona

Madrid could serve as the hub for this trip but Zaragoza would be better if possible. **Medinaceli** lies 155 kms. east of Madrid on the Barcelona highway. The view from the albergue at the edge of the cliff is unsurpassable. There is also a 3rd-century Roman arch, and sunsets and dawns that are extraordinary.

At Santa María de Huerta, 27 kms. east of Medinaceli, take a sharp right to the **Cistercian Foundation** begun in 1141 and finished in 1764. There you should see:

The *cloister,* the finest of its kind in Spain.

The *refectory* with its lectory and stairs set in the wall.

The *tremendous beard* of the brother who guides you about. Edward Lear's birds are certainly nesting in it.

Though it looks modern, **Zaragoza** has its Roman, Visigothic, and Arab history. There are two things you will want to see:

The *old cathedral,* built on the site of a mosque, with its remarkable octagonal dome.

The vast *new cathedral* (late 17th century), most effective when its ten blue-tiled cupolas are seen shining in the sun.

Zaragoza to Tudela. It is easily worth the round trip of 170 kms. to **Tudela** for a view of the west portal of the 13th-century collegiate church. It is profusely carved in an unsurpassable scene of the Last Judgment, in which there are one hundred and sixteen groups of figures. You have no notion at all of the medieval mind until you have seen what is happening to the damned at the right of this wonderful show. Required seeing—as also are the capitals in the cloister. One in particular cannot fail to endear itself to you. Lazarus is coming from his grave; his family in the foreground wear pleased smiles—but two of his friends in the background are holding their noses.

Zaragoza to the Pyrenees. First to Huesca, 72 kms. northeast, and then east 53 kms. to **Barbastro,** and you are at the take-off point for the grandest part of the Pyrenees. From here you can drive in almost any direction:

North, through the famous mountain village of **Ainsa** to **Boltana,** 74 kms.

North to the *Parque Nacional de Ordesa* and the National Parador Monte Perdido at Bielsa—if you want mountains. But reserve rooms well ahead.

To **Benasque** and the *Pico de Aneto,* tallest of the Pyrenean pack.

Huesca to Jaca. Loarre Castle: Northwest from Huesca 28 kms. on N240 is Ayerbe. Turn right 8 kms. to the one perfect castle of its age left in Europe. It was finished at the end of the 11th century, a castle-monastery of the Augustinian order. A superb fortress and church and a superb view. This you must see. The castle road has sharp hairpin turns. As you approach this area, the sheer beauty and peace of the place become ever more compelling.

South of Jaca 18 kms., a good gravel road turns left to the *Monastery of San Juan de la Peña,* St. John's of the Cliff. Eleventh-century Romanesque enclosing remnants of the 8th-century establishment, it is built inside a huge cavern in a red cliff at the head of a wild ravine. The pantheon of the early kings of Aragón, and the center of their first stand against the Arab conquerors, it is one of the sights of Spain.

At **Jaca** itself there is only the cathedral, with its interior and its carvings. Mainly you will use Jaca as a point of departure for the mountains and mountain valleys:

To **Canfranc, Valle de Aran** and **Canadanchu,** for summer and winter sports.

To **Baños de Panticosa,** one of the highest towns in Europe, for the water and mountain peaks.

To the **Valle de Hecho,** and the unusual village of **Hecho.**

To the **Valle de Ansó,** and the village of **Ansó,** where the people still practice a very ancient form of communism—the collective ownership of pastures and forests.

And then you are in **Navarra,** where you can either linger in glorious scenery, or drive straight to **Pamplona** and rest.

At this point your itinerary may be varied by touring the **Basque Provinces**—the *Vascongadas.* This green, fresh, somewhat rainy country is vacationland *par excellence,* in the midst of beautiful country and excellent cooking. Consult the Tourist Information Office in Pamplona for any number of delightful resorts, starting at the top with **San Sebastián.**

The present itinerary, however, takes you back to Zaragoza via Logroño and through splendid gorges and by an exceedingly steep pass, the *puerto de Piqueras*—call it the Onion Range—to **Sorio.**

In Soria you will want to see: The town itself, glowing and dark red; the fine sculpture of the west porch of *Santo Domingo;* the *closter of San Pedro,* in the middle of town. And most notably, the unique *cloister of San Juan de Duero,* across the river. You'll see nothing like it anywhere else.

From Soria, southeast to Calatayud and then east 177 kms. to Zaragoza.

ZARAGOZA TO VALENCIA VIA TERUEL AND SAGUNTO

Teruel took a terrible beating during the Civil War, but it has now nearly recovered. It has the finest assemblage of *mudéjar* towers and churches in Spain. Notice the great ceiling in the cathedral, hidden for centuries behind a false plaster vaulting, and so preserved.

The 142 kms. southeast from Teruel to Sagunto and the Mediterranean make a magnificent drive. In passing, see **Segorbe,** part 14th century.

Valencia is too well known by this time for the lyric description which it assuredly deserves. Half Moorish, one-quarter British, it is wholly Mediterranean. Climate and irrigation have made the *Huerta de Valencia* the most fertile land of all Spain, a perfumed land with orange and lemon groves along the coast, the lemon trees flowering even while they ripen their fruit.

There is much to see. Here is an abbreviated checklist:

The *cathedral,* with its "Palau" portal and its Miguelete tower, which has the only rich-sounding bell in all Spain. Climb the tower for a fine view of city, *huerta* and sea.

The 14th-century gate, the huge *puerta Serranos,* still scarred by French cannon shot; and its 15th-century counterpart, the *puerta Cuarte.*

The *Museum of Fine Arts,* one of the best in Spain.

The splendid Gothic buildings, the *Lonja* and *Consulado.*

The *Generalidad,* with its magnificent *Sala Dorada,* the Golden Hall, and its *Salón de Cortes,* Parliament Hall.

The port, called the *Grao.*

The famous *Fiesta de las Fallas,* if you happen to be there on March 19. Enormous papier-mâché sets on floats, and the sky in a torrent of flames from the fireworks display.

The *Tribunal de las Aguas,* the Water Tribunal, governing the control and use of the eight major canals of the irrigation system in the Huerta. Its reputation for justice has been formidable since its founding in the 10th century. Even though the judges are farmers, not lawyers, and no written records are ever made, its rulings are never questioned. The *Tribunal* convenes every Thursday, just before noon, at the Gate of the Apostles, the south portal of the cathedral.

VALENCIA TO ALICANTE

The coast line to the south is completely charming. Go left for **Denia** to see the castle and village, and to watch the coastal fishing vessels being built. The road to Denia has not been dug out to its present depth of five feet; 2,600 years of traffic have worn it down.

The **Peñon de Ifach,** the second Gibraltar of the Mediterranean, is a great spire of rock rising up out of the water offshore. Stay the night in the National Parador Costa Blanca on the Peñón itself. Nearby **Altea,** situated on a hilltop, is an artists' colony. Several shops offer ceramics, silver and paintings by local artists. The old town of **Callosa de Ensarria,** largely undiscovered, is also a haven for artists. Stop at the *Galeria Arabel* for paintings and prints by European and American artists. Excellent quality and value.

Further south, **Benidorm,** a popular resort, features modern hotels, night clubs and splendid, but crowded, beaches.

Alicante is a handsome oriental town with palm trees along the waterfront. Climb up to the towering heights of the *castle of Santa Barbara,* the only fortress along the Mediterranean coast that proved impregnable to Napoleon's invaders.

And finally, see the entirely African town of **Elche,** where the palms for Spanish Palm Sunday are grown, blessed, and distributed.

Four kms. north of Alicante on the coast, at San Juan, a road turns left into the mountains. The drive back to Valencia over this road will be one of the half-dozen memorable ones of your life. The 54 kms. to **Alcoy,** via **Jijona** are formidable. At the latter place you buy *turrones,* nougats made of almond or of hazelnut. From Alcoy you plunge eastward into a wild nest of mountains, heading toward **Guadalest** (31 kms.), a unique Arab town in and on top of an immense rock. From there east to the sea and back to Valencia.

About 150 kms. north, past Sagunto and Castellón is **Peñiscola,** one of the strangest towns in Europe. A huge, circular piston of rock stands up out of the sea offshore, connected to the land only by a narrow strip of sand. The houses stagger sharply upward to a massive castle built in the 13th century by the Knights Templar. Here it was that the schismatic pope, Benedict XIII, retired from Avignon with his court in the year 1415, and maintained his own papacy in the face of all Europe, until his death in the year 1423 at the age of ninety. Historically, visually, militarily, Peñiscola was and is inexpungeable.

A convenient 3 to 4 kms. to the north is the government parador at **Benicarló.** Delightful gardens, swimming pool and all.

At **Vinaroz,** 7 kms. north of Benicarló, a road takes you west directly toward Alcañiz, and from there 105 kms. to Zaragoza. **Barcelona,** your next objective, lies 300 kms. east, on the coast.

BARCELONA

Three hundred years ago Don Quixote described Barcelona as "unique both in beauty and situation." The second largest, the second wealthiest but to many, the most delightful city of Spain, it is inhabited by one of the briskest and most effervescent people of Europe. Without Barcelona's wealth, the Spanish government would have gone bankrupt annually these past four hundred years. The Cataláns know this. There is no love lost between them and Madrid.

Barcelona is a durable city. Founded by the Phocaean Greeks, it was taken by the Carthaginians about 237 B.C., and the first barbarian invasion overran it in 236 A.D. Reconquered by the Romans, it fell to the Arabs in 712, the Franks in 800.

First of all, take a little time in Barcelona to enjoy the atmosphere of the place. Stroll across the enormous Plaza de Cataluña, and then down the Ramblas to the port and La Barceloneta for great seafood. Walk that wonderful boulevard, the Passeig de Gracia, and shop for leather and ties and hats and books. Admire, if you can, the formidable examples along the Paseo of the work of the Catalán architect, Gaudí. Go on up to the Avinguda Diagonal, sit at the terrace of the "Parellada," have your *fino* and watch the world go by. Then, and only then, consider these tours of the city.

See the *old city* first: the *cathedral,* and the Roman remains about it; the tremendous 15th-century palaces of the *"Diputación"* and the *"Audiencia";* the interesting *"Museo de Historia de Barcelona";* the splendid *Plaza del Rey;* and *Plaza del Ángel,* where you find more of the Roman walls. Barcelona is spread out, so you will probably take a taxi to see the old churches of *Santa Mariá del Mar,* 10th century, *San Pedro de las Puellas* (twice burned, the last time in 1936, and twice restored), and *San Pablo del Campo.*

Go out the Gran Vía de les Corts Catalanes to the Plaza de España. There on the 1929 Exposition grounds you will find several very important museums, the most interesting and the boldest being the *Pueblo*

Español, Spanish Town, where within a replica of the walls of Ávila characteristic streets and houses of the provinces of Spain have been set up. This you must see. Then to the top of the hill called *Montjuich* for the view and for lunch *al fresco.* The food is fair, the view wonderful.

See the work of that extraordinary architect, Antoní Gaudí—the *Parque Güell* and the unfinished *Sagrada Familia* church. In neither place will you believe your eyes. Nevertheless, there the buildings are —icicles, stalagmites and all.

Go up Tibidabo, the mountain behind the city, for a superb view of the town and of the Mediterranean. At sunset Barcelona looks like a shining city buried under the sea.

Outside Barcelona are three trips you should take:

North on the Costa Brava. The Costa Brava, the Wild Coast, is for you if you like savage coast line, roads skirting the edge of cliffs above blue Mediterranean water, scores of beaches with towering mountains behind them, and little fishing villages that are reached only by bad roads.

From Barcelona to the French border (234 kms.), you pass a dozen towns, but the drive itself is the great attraction.

Tossa de Mar. See the old quarter and castle.

San Feliú de Guixols, with its 14th-century church, its tangle of white streets and its curio shops, is worth a stop.

S'Agaró, just beyond, is frankly a resort. The Hotel La Gavina is decisively *haute luxe.*

Palamós has a handsome broken coast line and a fine photogenic fishing fleet.

Palafrugell has both Roman remains and magnificent beaches: *Calella, Llafranch, Tamariú,* and *Aiguablava*—all so charming that you are likely to find them already crowded.

Bagur is a picturesque small village on top of a hill in an imposing cliffside setting.

La Escala is the home of the ruins of Ampurias, with Roman, Greek, and Visigothic elements.

Return to Barcelona inland via **Figueras,** stopping at **Gerona** for the

Gothic cathedral in Barcelona

Plaza de Cataluna in Barcelona

Tossa de Mar on the Costa Brava

night. The Hotel Peninsular is a colorful 19th-century museum piece. See the cathedral (the widest nave of any church in Christendom), the odd staircase streets, the cloister of *San Pedro de Galligáns,* St. Peter of Cock-Crow Brook, and, nearby, the "Arab" *baths.*

Inland from Barcelona. You can best explore the country behind Barcelona in short trips. Here are three examples.

Drive west some 40 kms. to **Montserrat,** Sawtooth Mountain, just off the Madrid highway. The monastery itself is nothing (though the Gregorian music turned out by its *Escolanía* is among the finest anywhere), but the mountain on which it is built is strange and fascinating. Walk up the precipitous trails or take the absolutely hair-raising ride via aerial cable to the top for a stupendous view.

Go west 70 kms. to Igualada, then northeast another 30 to Manresa, and finally north 32 more to **Cardona,** which has a spectacularly placed castle with one of the best of the Catalán Romanesque churches in it. Down below the castle is the incredible mountain of salt mentioned earlier. Just beyond Cardona is **Solsona,** with medieval atmosphere, a castle and walls, and an interesting Diocesan Museum. This is a comfortable day's run, with much of Spain in it.

Drive west on the Madrid highway 29 kms. to Martorell, then north 15 kms. to **Tarrasa.** Here you will see two early Romanesque churches and a Visigothic baptistery. In one of the churches, *Santa María,* is a wall painting of the murder of Thomas à Becket done three years after the event. A news flash, so to speak. Then southeast to **Rubi,** and on to **San Cugat del Vallés** for one of the famous cloisters of Spain.

Southwest from Barcelona. For a fine mountain drive, take the inland route to **Molíns del Rey** and **Villafranca del Panadés,** and from there southwest to the coast and Tarragona.

Tarragona. Drive up the hill past the new town to the old walls, which now have a circumference of two miles—though they are said to have once run nearly forty miles. The history of Tarragona begins there. The foundation stones, some of them measuring twelve feet in length and five in thickness, called "cyclopean," were somehow laid there by unknown people about the year 1000 B.C. The two Scipios took the town in 218 B.C. It became the capital of half of Spain. Julius Caesar embellished it. Augustus lived in it for two years and gave it a forum, a palace, a circus, baths, and temples. And if that is not enough, Pontius Pilate began his public service here.

You should see: the *walls;* the *praetorium;* the *amphitheater;* the *burial ground* and its *museum;* and the *aqueduct.*

There is also a convincingly medieval side to the city—the *cathedral.* In the cloister, don't miss the charming capital carving that, in a surprisingly modern style, tells the story of the rats carrying the dead cat to his grave, where he revives and devours his pallbearers.

North and west from Tarragona, 42 kms., is the monastery of **Poblet** an enormous place, rich in details that will make the medieval monks come to life for you. Most notable are the *church* and its royal *tombs,* and the *novices' dormitory,* a room about the length of a football field.

A few kilometers northeast is the monastery of *Santas Creus,* Holy Cross, almost as fine as Poblet, where King Pedro el Grande lies in his sepulcher—an enormous porphyry bathtub of Roman make.

You could see Tarragona and the two monasteries in a day. Better take two. You can return to Barcelona along the coast via the well-known resort, **Sitges.** Swim and eat pleasantly there, but in a great crowd.

THE BALEARIC ISLANDS: MALLORCA, MENORCA, IBIZA

For centuries, each generation has "discovered" the Balearics with the air of having stumbled over the Kohinoor diamond. When Caecilius Metellus, conqueror of the islands for Rome, returned home for his triumph, some elderly matron must surely have stifled a yawn and recalled Mallorca as it had been thirty years earlier, before it was quite spoiled.

Mallorca, the largest of the three islands, is only 45 miles one way and 60 the other, but it holds some 360,000 inhabitants, all somehow hidden out of sight—unless you go to Palma or to the popular beaches.

Mallorca is a matter of orange and lemon groves, of carob trees and palms, of harbors large and small. From 5,000-foot *Puig Mayor* in the north, the island slopes downward in the east and south to salt-pans and the sea. To the west you drive a hair-raising corniche road hundreds of feet above blue water, and on the east you may explore a dozen busy little harbors that only twenty years ago were lost to time. If it's

The hotel-lined shore front at Palma de Mallorca

rest and relaxation and escape you want, you'll find it in Mallorca.

Today the island is only a short hop from the mainland—by plane two hours from Paris, one and a half from Madrid, and thirty-five minutes from Barcelona or Valencia. By boat it is an overnight trip from either of the latter two places.

If you take the boat from Barcelona, you will arrive at Palma in the morning. The harbor itself is incredibly beautiful, and as you approach the docks, you will see at sunrise one of the great Gothic cathedrals of the world, an enormous and majestic 14th-century masterpiece standing broadly on its high terrace just at the water's edge.

In Palma you will spend much time at your hotel and the beaches, but you can also mingle fine sight-seeing with your sybaritic pleasures. Here is a checklist of high lights:

Next to the cathedral, the *Almudaina,* what is left of the Moorish fortress. And also Moorish, the *Arab baths* at No. 15 calle de la Serra.

The striking early-14th-century castle of *Bellver,* the only large circular castle in existence. A taxi will spare you most of the stiff, hot hill, but you'll have to climb the circular stair to the tower on your own. It is worth every twinge for the view along the coast and over the almond groves below.

The *Lonja,* an extremely handsome Gothic civic edifice.

The *market,* a colorful display of vegetables, fish and animals for the table, every morning at the *Plaza Mayor.*

But Palma is only part—and not the best part—of Mallorca. You can also drive southwest past the elegant beach resorts to Andraitx and then take the cliff-hanger drive to Valldemosa, in its almond orchards, where George Sand and Chopin once spent several violent and well-publicized months.

Driving east you will pass through Manacor, with its 18th-century towers and its medieval air, on your way to the *Caves of Artá* and *Drach.* The former is more exquisite in its coloring. But the latter boasts a strange unearthly lake where you may go boating—or hear a water-borne concert.

As for the rest, the island is so small that you can hardly avoid the half-dozen unique and colorful towns you should see: Inca, Sóller, Banalbufar, Pollensa, Andraitx, Valldemosa, Manacor. If rest and tranquillity are your objectives, you will seek out Formentor, Pollensa, Cala Ratjada, Camp de Mar, Patuera, Andraitx, Puerto de Alcudia, Porto-Cristo, and Cala d'Or.

Menorca and **Ibiza,** second and third in size of the Balearic Islands, have in the past twenty years become increasingly popular. You go to them for the beaches, small boat sailing, and for an even more remote tranquillity than Mallorca offers. They are both charming, but they are not as untouched and untroubled as they once were. The relative cheapness of houses, of servants and of food has attracted great numbers of people who have found them an almost perfect escape.

NORTHWEST
TO GALICIA

The towering Roman aqueduct at Segovia

Vacationers spill over the French border into the Basque country, and as far as the central Cantábrican coast, all of which is splendidly equipped for holiday pleasures. But the northwest of Spain is visited by fewer tourists than the rest of the country. It is a pity that most people miss one of the most interesting areas of Spain. However limited your time, don't make that mistake.

Burgos is your first objective. Aranda de Duero, 160 kms. north of Madrid, brings you to a convenient midway point for lunch at the *Hostal Landa.* (But make a point of arriving early enough to reserve your table, since it is well patronized, particularly in summer.)

Due north past **Lerma** (impressive on its high rock but not worth exploring) is Burgos. Forty years ago it was pure Spanish, heavy with the spirit of old Castile. During the Civil War, however, it became the capital of Franquist Spain, and out of necessity, an industrial town. In a strictly Spanish sense, it became large, wealthy and modern.

But there are still many remains of the old Burgos: the imposing 14th-century *puerta de Santa María;* the *puerta de San Esteban,* an Arab gate in a fragment of the old walls; the *Casa de Miranda* with its handsome patio and staircase; the *Casa del Cordón,* so called because of the enormous Franciscan cord carved about the doorway—a doorway through which Columbus passed to report to Ferdinand and Isabella on the success of his second voyage; and, of course, the *cathedral.*

Most important is the cathedral, one of the landmarks of Spain. Begun in 1222, and consecrated in 1296, it was centuries more in building. The earlier part was in the French and English style, but in 1442, Hans of Cologne, whom the Spanish call Juan de Colonia, finished the towers and spires. After him, Simón de Colonia added the remarkable Chapel of the High Constable. Diego Siloé executed the gem of the entire collection, the Escalera Dorada, the Gilded Stairs. And in 1567, Juan de Vallejo finished the last of it, the *cimborium.*

The Spanish permit themselves a certain excess of enthusiasm about the cathedral, but others may find it confusing in its mixture of styles. Nevertheless, there are beautiful things here. The side aisles are plain but grandly conceived. The 14th-century choir stalls are splendidly carved, and the two organs are superb when in full voice. The crossing, richly ornamented though it may be, is so high and so well proportioned that ornament is lost in structure. The *Chapel of the High Constables of Castile* has always been highly praised, and it richly deserves it.

On a different plane is the *Escalera Dorada,* the Gilded Stairs, the finest work of art in the cathedral, executed by Diego Siloé, son of the sculptor Gil. And on still another level is the popular *Papa-moscas,* from *Atrapa-moscas,* meaning Fly-catcher. He is a mechanical figure stationed high up against the western wall, and his function is to sound the hours of his clock, which he does by pulling a rope. Simultaneously he opens and closes his mouth, thus catching his flies. From this stems an ancient custom of the town: on New Year's Eve, just before midnight, the *plaza mayor* is crowded with the Burgalese, all with bunches of grapes in their hands. At the first stroke of the hour the people shout *"Uno!"* and pop a grape into their mouths. At the second, *"Dos!"* and in goes another grape—and so on until the New Year has been properly and completely brought in.

You should not leave Burgos until you have seen the *Cartuja de Miraflores,* a Carthusian monastery founded in 1441. The Order is still in residence there, and if you put your ear to the cloister door, you can hear the only words the brethren are permitted to speak outside of the *locutorium, "¡Tenemos que morir!" "Ya lo sabemos."* "We must die!" "We already know it!"

But your purpose here is to see the work of Gil de Siloé, who carved the astonishing retable and the tombs of Don Juan II of Castilla, his wife, Doña Isabel of Portugal, and the Infante, Don Alfonso. It is almost beyond belief that alabaster be carved so minutely and delicately as to imitate to the last thread the richly patterned fabrics worn by the king and queen lying there before the altar. Of its kind, Siloé's sculpture here is pre-eminent in the world.

Santo Domingo de Silos. Southeast of Burgos 75 kms., in the heart of a green valley between mile-high mountains, is the village of **Silos,** and *Santo Domingo Monastery.*

Founded in the last years of the 6th century, the monastery was overrun by the Arabs, rebuilt in the 10th century, and again destroyed by the Arabs. Domingo, a Benedictine later to be canonized, began the third house in 1040. It received an unfortunate face-lifting in the 17th century, and in the following two centuries other changes were made. But happily, reconstruction money gave out in 1816, just before "work" was to have begun on the great cloister. In 1880 a French Benedictine community at Solesmes took over, restored the ancient house, and is still in residence there.

Remember as you look at the cloister, that but for a fortunate lack

The Cathedral of Burgos   *Interior of the Burgos Cathedral*

of money all this would have been destroyed. It is untouched Romanesque of the early 12th century, perhaps the most beautiful in all Europe. In any language, in any terms, here is great sculpture—Graeco-Roman, medieval, modern—intelligible to anyone through all the centuries it has existed.

BURGOS TO SANTANDER OR SANTILLANA DEL MAR

The road north winds up toward *Puerto del Escudo,* Shield Pass, a mounting climax of Alpine scenery that will leave your nerves twanging. Abruptly you arrive at the summit, and the road drops steeply into a glory of incredibly green grass. You have crossed to the west side of the range.

Here you must choose between **Santander** and **Santillana del Mar.** If you turn toward Santander, you will probably follow east along the coast of the Bay of Biscay to **San Sebastián.** Both cities are for holidaymakers. Santander's fine beach *el Sardinero,* is matched by San Sebastián's *la Concha,* and between them are dozens of smaller beaches sloping gently out to sea along the lovely coast. In all this area, you simply look at and use the sea and the mountains for rest and recreation. And you will find every holiday facility, for here are experts who have for generations practiced the art of catering to travelers.

But Santillana del Mar—"Santa Juliana" as pronounced in the local manner—is an excursion back into the Middle Ages. Santillana is the most impressive medieval town in Europe, scarcely retouched, simply itself as it was four hundred years ago. Even the National Parador Gil Blas—this was that amiable rogue's home town—in no way detracts from the effect; it is housed in one of the handsomest palaces. The rough-cobbled street and lanes, the two fountains that have been in use for over a millennium, the smell of passing cows, and the fumes of charcoal fires—all is medievality.

Even a movie house is banned by the government. The maids at the *parador* take this to heart and groan with the boredom of the Middle Ages. They say, "There's nothing here at all, not even a *paseo!* Only the *paseo de las vacas!*"—meaning the herds of cows that come through the street morning and evening.

The architectural glory of the place is the *collegiate church* and its cloister, built at the turn of the 12th century. Even those who don't fancy churches will like this one. It is one of the finest Romanesque in the north, with the exception of the cathedral at Santiago. The cloister is among the best in the country. And behind the silver frontal of the altar is an ageless polychromed mouse nibbling at the polychromed book of an unobservant St. Matthew.

Only a kilometer or so from the town is the *Cave of Altamira* which is open to the public on a limited basis. A letter requesting permission to visit the cave should be submitted far in advance, specifying dates preferred and the number in your party to: Director, Centro de Investigación y Museo de Altamira; Santillana del Mar (Santander), (Tel.: 81-81-02 and 81-80-05). Tourists can visit a museum at the entrance of the cave, which is open daily, and you will have an eerie sense of having reached beyond the beginning of history.

West of Santillana del Mar, the coastal road runs through little fishing villages to Gijón and thence to Oviedo, a modern and progressive city with little to see. Rather than delay there, you should go south to the government *parador* that bestrides the mile-high *Puerto de Pajares.* From any window you look out and down upon an astonishing depth of mountains. Sunrise and sunset there are spectacles that are easily worth the run of 53 kms. from Oviedo.

Downhill 55 kms. to the south is **León,** in Roman times an important city. Now its prestige rests on three things: 1. the fact that in León, in the year 1188, the first officially constituted parliament of Europe, the *cortes,* was convened; 2. the venerable *crypt* of the Romanesque church of *San Isidoro,* the great Visigothic saint and scholar; 3. the *cathedral.*

Santa María de Regla, the cathedral, is actually a towering roof over a vast, magnificent house of 13th- and 14th-century glass. The total area of these glass walls approximates 1200 square yards, and some of the windows are forty feet high. The slender stone ribs supporting the vault are all but invisible, drowned in the wash of fire from the flaring reds and glowing yellows, the greens, and rare purples. Santa María on a sunny day is absolutely unforgettable.

After León there is the usual choice: Do you want beautiful coast line? Then you return to Oviedo and follow the good road west. Mountains? Then you head to Astorga and from there on the main highway through Ponferrada and **Lugo**—the latter a town completely encircled by Roman walls.

On the coastal route your first stop in Galicia will probably be the handsome National Parador of Ribadeo, 174 kms. west of Oviedo. On the inland route, the old Pilgrim Way to Santiago, you must drive to Lugo, some 240 kms. from León, to find a place for the night.

Galicia is a labyrinth of harsh mountains. The *Gallego* is undeniably poor, but you would never guess it. Farms and vineyards and pastures are lush, the towns busy with coastal and deep-water commerce and endlessly engaged in harvesting their one great crop—fish.

In May and June, and again in September and October, Galicia is beautiful. As for the rain—or drizzle or fog—there it is, and you accept it, as you do in Scotland, stoutly saying nothing about it. You will remember only the vistas along the mountain roads, the air filled with the aroma of heath plants and the wild rose called *francesilla*. And you have never seen mountain walls so completely dressed in gala colors as when, after the vintage—the wines are light and very pleasant—the vine leaves on the terraces turn ocher-yellow and scarlet, as far down as the diminished string of the river, as high up as the granite rim that lets in the sky.

La Coruña is completely charming, a delightful mermaid emerging occasionally from rain and mist to dry off. (The inhabitants insist that August is utter desiccation, but this is only relative.) You may pause here for: the *old town,* the *ciudad Alta;* the *Roman lighthouse,* the only one in the world still functioning; and the typical glassed-in balconies

Interior of the Cathedral of León   *The crypt of San Isidoro in León*

characteristic of the town. But beyond all of these is simply the perva-
sive and indefinable charm of the town.

West from La Coruña through Carballo, along the rim of Cape
Finisterre, the ride becomes an odd mixture of the squealing ox-carts
of peasants and little boats putting out from fishing villages. Especially
notable among many such port towns is Muros, a town where the
women are traditionally so beautiful that the Barbary pirates came
there regularly on shopping expeditions, as it were. And **Noya,** founded
by Noah himself and so given his name. Further south is **Cambados,**
with its 17th-century town houses, notably the *Palacio de los Fefiñanes.*
Nearby **La Toja,** a charming little island, is a most elaborate and
haut-luxe place to put up for a rest. **Vigo** is famous for its cookery.
Take the drive around the peninsula of Domayo, and the boat ride out
to the islands of **Cíes** and its three monasteries.

Almost at the center of the circular tour you have just made is
Santiago de Compostela, St. James of the Field of the Star. From that
moment in the 9th century when the star was reported to have shone
over St. James' body, until the end of the 16th century, when the
making of pilgrimages began to wane, the cockle shell of St. James of
Compostela, symbol of a pilgrimage to Santiago, was more sought after
than the cross received by pilgrims at Jerusalem, or the emblem of
Rome. During those centuries hundreds of thousands passed under the
Pórtico de la Gloria to the high white altar of the *capilla mayor,* above
which towered the huge, seated statute of the saint. All this is still there.
You may still see a pilgrim or two approach the red granite cape, and
kiss the hem now worn thin by pilgrims before him. Santiago is a
medieval phenomenon.

Here you will do well to engage one of the many competent guides.
Make sure that you see in detail Mateo's great *Pórtico de la Gloria,* one
of the glories of Romanesque sculpture in Europe, and in particular,
the appealing face of the Prophet Daniel; the *Pórtico de la Plateria,*
especially the beautiful carving in the figure of King David at work on
his unusual harp; and the north portal, the *Fachada de la Azabachería,*
so called because here were the shops that sold the little jet figures of
the saint to the pilgrims.

Walk about the streets at night, particularly the *Rúa del Villar,* and
the *Rúa Nueva.* You will find yourself transported back thousands of
centuries. At the Hostal de Los Reyes Católicos (without much question, one of the most royal hotels in Europe), you are still with the
ghostly company, for this was the tremendous hospital established for
pilgrims by Isabella and Ferdinand.

FROM GALICIA TO ZAMORA AND SALAMANCA

Leaving the northwest through **Orense,** you skirt the border of
Portugal for 173 kms. through fine mountains to **Puebla de Sanabria**

Pórtico de la Gloria, façade and towers, Cathedral of Santiago de Compostela

where you can put up at the National Parador. Here you may walk up to the picturesque old town on its rock, or take a short drive north to the lake of Sanabria, which has enormous trout in its cold waters—the immediate reason for the enormous albergue. You are out of the mountains now and once more on the immense plains of Castile. A run of a little more than 100 kms. brings you down to Zamora.

Zamora is historic. Alfonso el Católico took the city from the Moors in 748 and built seven concentric walls about it. Almanzor leveled them in 985. Though later rebuilt, they now stand only in broken sections on the red hill, and the city stays within their ancient mold. It has great atmosphere.

Among many excellent examples of Romanesque, Zamora has two of note: the church of *La Magdalena,* a Templar construction of the 12th century, with one of the most unusual portals in Spain, a fine nave, and an exceptional tomb. And the *cathedral,* a striking 12th-century affair. Inside are two rarities: the magnificent *choir stalls* and the *misericordia seats,* carved by Rodrigo Alemán, who did similar ones at Plasencia and Ciudad Rodrigo. His capacity for satire, homely tales, and impropriety equaled his skill as a sculptor. All three cathedrals are full of thoroughly unchurchly episodes, such as the vivid carving here of a woman receiving a clyster in public.

Salamanca is not only one of the most gravely and elegantly beautiful cities in Europe; it is undoubtedly one of the most enchanting of university towns. In the 14th century, its university ranked second only to the one in Paris, and by the 16th century it numbered seven thousand students from all over the world. Columbus came there to seek support, and though the faculty of astronomy and mathematics let him down, Fra Diego de Deza and the Dominicans of San Esteban supported him against the Doctores, who had called his plan "vain, impracticable, and resting on grounds too weak to merit the support of Government." Now aside from the persistence of thirty or forty young Irish priests in attendance at the College of Irish Nobles and perhaps a few other scholars, the University is dead, and with it the city.

Salamanca with its golden walls and domes and turrets is to be seen as a whole. After an hour's walk through its streets, you will find that the particulars are absorbed in the great golden aura in which the 16th century is established here once more. The splendid *plaza mayor* makes you seem an outright anachronism. The *Casa de las Conchas* (the cockle shells of the pilgrim again), the *Torre del Clavero,* the buildings of the University—all of these become merely parts of the Salamanca experience. And when you cross the river on the Roman bridge and see the golden reflection of Salamanca in the River Tormes, you will fix its image forever in your memory.

Just as travelers rarely see the northwest, so do they seldom go anywhere in the west save to Salamanca. And yet it happens that only 87 kms. southwest of Salamanca is one of Spain's most unusual cities, **Ciudad Rodrigo.**

By all means go to Ciudad Rodrigo. The walled town wears its ancient history with a quiet, provincial grace; the *plaza mayor,* a 17th-century triumph, is a costume piece. The narrow streets, pressed between imposing 16th- and 17th-century town houses, suddenly open out into charming arcaded squares where the blazing sun is tamed by polled trees, or plunge into abrupt tunnels where the gates of the town bore through the heavy city walls. You may sit in the garden of the *parador,* one of Spain's handsomest, and look over into Portugal, or you may take the sentry walk along the city walls to the *cathedral.* You should take that walk for two reasons:

The *choir stalls,* on which Rodrigo Alemán lavished his skill and audacity. One of his unmentionable monsters has for centuries served the canons as a hand grip for hoisting themselves into the first tier of stalls. The *misericordia* shows three monks at service, clad to their necks in wine-skins; the book from which they are singing is carved with a few musical notations and the words, "Vino puro," pure wine.

Your second reason for being here lies in the carvings in the *cloister.* Around the columns are perched miniature rabbits; a tiny frog plays his lute; a little naked figure has slumped face forward asleep; an artist sits to his work, holding a palette. Best of all, a miniature monk lies on his back asleep, his book of prayers on his chest and his feet cocked up against the foot of the column.

Cáceres, about 150 kms. south, has many memories, Roman and Arab and Christian Spanish. The modern town is merely surprising. But the old town on the hill is worth walking through, to see the famous *tower of Abul-Jacob;* the *Moorish walls* at the Arco de la Estrella, the *Arch of the Star;* and the houses of the 17th-century hidalgos who returned from the new colonies loaded with gold: the *Casa de las Veletas,* the *Casa del Sol,* the *Casa de los Becerra.*

Northwest of Cáceres 62 kms. is the Roman bridge of **Alcantara,** called by the Arabs *Alcantara-as-Saif,* the Bridge of the Sword. It is one of the half dozen great Roman sights left in the world. The figures themselves are impressive: length, about two hundred yards; width, about eight; maximum height above the normal water level, about one hundred and ninety feet. From the Tajo gorge the sight is utterly overwhelming.

Mérida lies 70 kms. south of Cáceres. Here you must remind yourself that the Roman city founded in 15 B.C. was three times the size of the present city. An excitable and perhaps unreliable Visigothic chronicler reported that Mérida once had eighty-four gates and five castles and that its towers numbered three thousand seven hundred.

The bridge at Mérida, over half a mile in length, is Rome's longest. Along the north bank is the massive *alcázar,* of Roman stone but of Arab workmanship. Within the heavy walls now are vegetable gardens, orchards, and workshops—and the original cistern of the fortress, with its Roman steps. To the north of the *plaza mayor,* you will find the voussoirs of the massive *Arch of Trajan.* Down the road is the blurred oval of the *Circus Maximus,* over four hundred yards long and one hundred wide. The *theater* and *amphitheater,* both in a fair state of preservation, are much more impressive, and do more than anything else in Mérida to re-establish its Roman atmosphere and prestige.

Out along the road to Salamanca—the Roman *Via de la Plata*— across a handsome Roman bridge, are the remains of one of the three aqueducts which once supplied the city. A little way beyond, unimpaired and still capable of functioning after 2,000 years, is the reservoir that fed this aqueduct.

SOUTHWEST
TO
ANDALUCIA

Seville's two landmarks—Cathedral and Giralda Tower

Andalucía was the first Spanish kingdom to enter history, a thousand years before our era. It contained within itself the empire of Tartesos, a flourishing Roman civilization, and the whole cycle of Spanish Islam. Yet little is left of all this.

The Moorish south offers the Mediterranean coast, the great range of the Sierra Nevada, and a few cities to spend some time in: **Seville, Córdoba, Granada, Ronda, Úbeda.** Many other towns, rich and golden, can be seen almost in passing: **Carmona, Écija, Arcos de la Frontera, Vejer de la Frontera, Medina Sidonia, Álora, Baeza.**

Seville. It is amazing that Seville has managed somehow to survive a century and a half of musical, sentimental, jasmine-scented praise— Mozart's *Don Giovanni,* Rossini's *Barber of Seville,* and Bizet's *Carmen.* It still suffers under an annual flood of words and pictures when Holy Week comes around. But even more astonishing is the fact that Seville still remains fascinating, communicating its gaiety impartially to all who see the city, fully justifying the adulation they give it. It has more special character than any other city in Spain.

Seville appeared first as an Iberian town called Híspalis, and later came into favor with Julius Caesar during his war with Pompey. After Rome fell, it became the Visigothic capital. In 1248 San Fernando Rey made it the seat of the royal court. Seville's wealth and power increased enormously and continued to grow after Columbus landed there from his first voyage, and the city was given the monopoly of the New World trade. Although some fifty-five miles inland on the Guadalquivir, Seville is still an active, deep-water port.

Seville, it is evident, is not a one-dimensional city. No brief guide will reveal its essence or illuminate its charm. What follows is only an enumeration of charms that have never yet been adequately described.

For an introductory survey, climb to the top of the great *Giralda tower,* the minaret of the city's principal mosque and one of the most splendid towers you'll ever see. You go up by a ramp, which is easier than steps: but Ibn Yusuf, who had the tower built (1184–96) had it easiest of all. He rode his horse up the three hundred and five feet.

The *cathedral,* one of the largest in Christendom, was begun in 1402, completed two hundred years later, damaged by earthquakes and restored again as late as 1901. Take a guide or join a party. There's no other way of managing these huge cathedrals. The retable of the High Altar is probably the artistic climax of the place, and the tomb of Columbus the historical one.

The *Patio de los Naranjos,* the Court of the Orange Trees, belonging to the old mosque. Off this lies the *Biblioteca Colombina,* where you may see Columbus' manuscripts.

The *Alcázar,* built for the Almohade king, Abu Yakob, in 1181, added to by Pedro el Cruel, Henry II, Isabella, Charles I, and several others. This palace-castle is very nearly as fine as the Alhambra, and in a pinch will take its place in your book.

The *gardens of the Alcázar.*

The *Muelle,* the port, by the bridge to Triana on the other side of the river.

Two remarkable palaces done in the Moorish *mudéjar* manner, astonishingly rich in carving, woodwork, and tiles: the *Casa de Pilato,* of the early fifteen hundreds; and the *Casa de las Dueñas,* built a few years earlier. The *gardens* of the latter are especially fine.

The façade of the church of *Santa Paula,* a remarkable creation in glazed and colored tile. Also the magnificent ceiling of the church of *Santa Clara.*

The *Museo Provincial* and the *Hospital de la Caridad,* for some of the best paintings of Zurbarán and Ribera, and for the Murillos that unquestionably mark that painter as great.

The *Fábrica de los Tabacos,* simply for old time's sake, to commemorate the first performance you ever heard of *Carmen.*

The *Parque María Luisa,* and the *Paseo de las Delicias,* for relaxation and lunch.

A table at the western approach to the famous *Sierpes* street, to have the *Sevillano* drink, *manzanilla,* and to observe the astonishing animation of the citizenry.

A horse-drawn cab for a tour of the old quarter of the town, the *Barrio de Santa Cruz.* Not to be described. You must see it.

A run north to **Santiponce** and the Roman ruins of *Italíca.*

A visit to a *café cantante* recommended by a knowledgeable citizen, or by your *concierge,* for *flamenco* singing and dancing.

One warning only: Don't try to drive about the central part of Seville. You'll never come untangled, never emerge.

SEVILLE TO CÓRDOBA

In 33 kms. you come to **Carmona.** Just before the town is a Roman necropolis (2nd century B.C.—4th century A.D.): subterranean tombs, nine hundred of them, some of them the size of houses, one with a two-storied patio. You will also want to see the massive Roman-Arab gate, the *puerta de Sevilla,* and, as you flank the city, the Arab *alcázar.*

Córdoba. Time has been unkind to Córdoba. In the 9th and 10th centuries it was the Athens of the west, the only light in Europe. But when that light was extinguished, Córdoba did not have the good fortune to fall into decay in tranquillity. In the 11th century it was sacked and burned no less than four times, and when the Reconquest arrived, it was a deserted town.

And Córdoba fell to this from true magnificence. In the 10th century, it was a city of 800,000 inhabitants, 300 mosques, twice that many public baths, and 600 inns. Two palaces—it is no exaggeration to call them gigantic—were built during that century, *Medina az-Zahra,* by Abd-er-Rahman III, and *az-Zahira,* by Almanzor. But in 1020, both these palaces were destroyed.

Think for a moment of these details of *Medina az-Zahra,* the lesser building. Nearly a mile long and almost half a mile wide, it took forty years to construct with 10,000 workmen, 2,400 mules and 400 camels.

Archways in the interior of the Mosque in Córdoba

It contained 4,000 marble columns, 1,500 doors sheathed with copper leaf, and—Abd-er-Rahman's special fancy—a large pool filled with quicksilver.

Miraculously, the great mosque escaped damage until Charles I gave the ecclesiastical authorities permission to set up a cathedral within its very precincts. When he later saw what had been done, he is reported to have said, "If I had known what you were up to, you would never have done it. What you have made here can be found anywhere, and what you have destroyed exists nowhere else." Nevertheless, the mosque survives as one of the great buildings of the West.

The *mosque* is obviously your first objective. You will be aware of the eight hundred and fifty columns—merely as a marble forest. The archway and ceiling of the *Capilla Real* and the *Capilla de Villaviciosa* are wonderful enough. But the *mihrab*—where the mosque's copy of the Koran was kept, and where the devout ended their pilgrimage by walking seven times about the walls—is the glory of the mosque. Its arabesque ornament and its mosaic are splendid.

The *bridge* over the Guadalquivir is the most conspicuous memento of the Roman occupation.

There are lesser Moorish remains. The *bell towers* of the churches of *Santiago* and *San Juan de los Caballeros* are minarets, later crowned by a Christian arrangement for bell ringing. (The Moors detested the interminable noise of the Christians' bells.)

The *Moorish bath,* the only one of the six hundred left, in the *calle de los Baños,* the Street of the Baths.

A beautiful *synagogue* of the early 14th century in the *barrio judio,* the Jewish quarter. Notable for its plaster carving.

The *church of San Pedro,* conspicuous for the grace of its west front and for the maniacal enthusiasm of the baroque decoration in its *Capilla de los Martines.* The rose window of *San Lorenzo* is rarely beautiful and *San Agustín* has a charming facade and interior.

All of these you should see. And what Córdoba once was you should remember.

SEVILLE TO JEREZ DE LA FRONTERA, TARIFA, CÁDIZ

It is a run of 101 kms. south from Seville to **Jerez de la Frontera.** Jerez is sherry, so mispronounced by the English tongue. Spend a day in the city for the pure joy of it; if you're there in Holy Week or the *Vendimia* (the vintage in mid-September), stay longer, because Jerez is in a wonderful mood then. The city is Andalusian with an odd overtone that you won't identify until you learn that since the great sherry *bodegas* have been heavily Anglicized during the past century, there are English comforts and ways and speech here and there. But Andalucía asserts itself in the white houses, the sidewalks shaded by orange trees, the bars and cafés with their uncountable variety of sherry wines.

You should also visit one of the *bodegas,* of which "González Byass" is the greatest. The courtesy of Don Manuel and his staff is not to be surpassed anywhere, nor is the quality of his wines.

Southeast of Jerez 35 kms. over a poor road is **Medina Sidonia,** an incandescently white Moorish town astride a hill in the middle of wild, unvisited country. Notice the *Arab gate* as you enter, and the *Roman funeral statue* embedded in the corner of a house on your right as you go down the principal street. Forty or fifty kms. south there suddenly appears above the rolling mountains a shape familiar to you—the *Rock of Gibraltar,* even more dramatic from the land side than from the sea. Before you is the Bay of Algeciras and Algeciras itself. From there you may take a boat across to the Rock.

The short, high run southwest to **Tarifa** gives you an impressive view of the Atlas Mountains across the Straits in Africa and of the other one of the Pillars of Hercules.

Tarifa achieves an African air with its Moorish walls and city gate of the horseshoe style, and the quite well preserved 14th-century *castle of Guzmán el Bueno,* the Duke of Medina Sidonia.

Northwest from Tarifa the road is flat and un-Spanish, running along beside the Atlantic and its long beaches. One conspicuous exception: a very tall pinnacle of rock, and on top of it the impregnable town of **Vejer de la Frontera.** Go up and walk about. It merits the adjective "picturesque."

Another 50 kms. north, past the gleaming salt-pans of San Fernando, on a slender neck of the little peninsula, is **Cádiz,** blue and white and delicate, noted now only for its *flamenco* dancing and quiet charm. But 2,000 years ago, Tartessians, Carthaginians, Romans, and later Arabs and the explorers of the New World, found it less than quiet. Its history is now invisible—the Temple of Hercules and the lighthouse over-thrown into the Atlantic by an emir of Niebla in the 12th century, and the old city sacked and fired by Essex in 1596.

JEREZ DE LA FRONTERA TO RONDA

From Jerez to Ronda you will be launched on one of the half dozen great drives of your life. East of Jerez where the Guadalete meanders through the sunlit, fertile valley, you will see within the half-circle of one of its turns, a spine of rock heaved up to a height of five hundred feet. On it are the white houses and the gray palaces of **Arcos de la Frontera,** a village that the noted Spanish journalist Azorín considered the most beautiful of all Spain. Go up its steep streets to the *plaza mayor;* go to the edge of it and look down the cliff to the river. When you drive on around the base, stop to look up through the eucalyptus trees. You might well find yourself agreeing with Azorín.

From Arcos to **Ronda** via C344 is 96 rugged kilometers through the Serranía de Ronda. These mountains are never more than a mile high, but they shimmer like hard steel and their flanks are steep. You drive in and out of a wild confusion of jagged peaks, climbing incessantly until that moment when the road stops abruptly and far below you see the huge hollow bowl from which rises the rocky shaft of Ronda.

But before you reach your objective there are two grand moments. The first is the sight of **Grazalema,** in the heart of its special massif. Your road goes on, leading straight up out of the village, clinging to the high mountain walls as if frightened out of its wits—and it has plenty of reason to feel so—on to the high, vertiginous, ledge-clinging, white, impregnable Arab village of **Zahara.** This too is a memorable sight. And the rest of the way to Ronda is no anticlimax.

Ronda. Boost a mile-wide, flat-topped cylinder of rock a thousand feet up from a 40-kilometer circular plain; surround it by mountains; set an impossible town upon the edge of it; split the town and the rock with a sheer-sided gorge 200 feet wide and 350 feet deep; span this gorge with an impossible bridge with a central arch that reaches from river bed to the top of the rock—and you have **Ronda.**

Put up at the *Reina Victoria Hotel.* Walk out to the parapet of its front garden, take a deep breath, and look over. There are greater depths, to be sure, but you won't be thinking of that fact just then. If it's toward evening, the enormous vultures of the *Serranía* will be

Cliffside houses at Ronda   *A bridge at Ronda*

Pool in the gardens of the Alhambra   *Court of the Lions in the Alhambra*

mounting the thermal currents from the plain below, sweeping on motionless wings up the face of the precipice, and with a noiseless rush swirling away just above your head.

Ronda has been important for two centuries, and for two reasons. The first is that it is a center for the raising of horses, mules and bulls. It has the oldest bull ring in Spain (18th century) and is the venerated capital of *tauromaquía*. The second is that for the same number of years the city has been clearing house and center for contraband out of Gibraltar, an industry that goes well with the landscape.

RONDA TO GRANADA VIA MÁLAGA

It has been said that Málaga has the soul of a garden. She also has the soul of a fish, twenty thousand annual tons of most delicious small fish. Between fish and flowers and an extraordinarily bland climate, the city is a dream come true. As for the soul of the garden: everywhere and every day, the streets of Málaga are a flower market—roses, jasmine, carnations, camellias, violets and orange and lemon blossoms. The park along the waterfront is a glorious half-mile riot of flowers and trees unmatched anywhere on this side of the Mediterranean.

The soul of the fish? Expressed in a dozen different ways of expressing the soul of hake, of sardines, of red mullet, of tuna—which runs in fair abundance on either side of the Straits—and, most notably, anchovy, the *boquerón.* Tied by the tails into sets of five, fresh from the sea and the frying, these are indescribably good. And, at night, the sight of hundreds of lighted boats out to catch all these fish—that is a sight to see.

Lunch at the *Parador Nacional de Gibralfaro* on the hill below the Moorish castle, the *Alcazaba.* The food is excellent, the view of Málaga and its bull ring and its shining sea equally so.

Eastward from Málaga you are launched upon still another triple-starred drive. The 109 kms. over the corniche road to **Motril** (and on to Almería, for that matter) are formidable. But you are heading for **Granada,** so you turn north at Motril.

In Granada you will find the *Capilla Real,* the Royal Chapel, next to the cathedral, where behind a magnificent grill of forged iron are the sumptuously carved tombs of Ferdinand and Isabella. Behind the effigies are the steps leading down to the crypt where, in plain leaden coffins, lie the bodies of the two great rulers who with their conquest of the Moors brought the Middle Ages to a close in Spain.

The scope of history is staggering here. In the minds of the two monarchs as they rode toward the walls of Granada in January of 1492 must have reverberated the names of the long line of kings and captains who had struggled to drive Islam out of Spain. To recapture Spain had been an article of faith for nearly eight centuries. And still Islam had not received a mortal stroke. Though the Moors had lost Valencia, Toledo, Seville, and Córdoba, for two hundred and fifty years the Nazari dynasty had held the powerful and wealthy kingdom of Granada. But now Granada had fallen. Isabella was profoundly moved. By reliable report, as she rode from Santa Fé to Granada that morning in early January, she could not speak to anyone but kept repeating, *"Non nobis, Domine, non nobis . . ."* It was inconceivable! Granada had fallen! The seemingly endless history of Islam, full of honor and glory and distinction, had come to an end.

At the head of the first column of the Christian army before the walls of Granada were Ferdinand and Isabella, both in armor. Boabdil rode out of the gate with a dozen courtiers, all of them in mourning. He dismounted and made his ceremonial abasement first to the king and afterward to Isabella. Meanwhile Don Guitierre, the Comendador of León, surrounded by the high rank of church and army, mounted to the top of the *Torre de la Vela,* the tallest one of the Alhambra, while cannon fired volleys of celebration. Then simultaneously a great silver cross and the standard of the Knights of Santiago and the royal standards of Castile and Aragon were raised three times, while a royal herald cried out the words that are repeated in the ceremony that annually commemorates the surrender: *"¡Granada, Granada, Granada! Por los muy altos y poderosos reyes, Don Fernando y Doña Isabel, nuestros señores!"*

Thus ended the venture begun by Tarik in the year 711. Every day in Granada at three o'clock in the afternoon the bell of the Plegaria Tower strikes three times, to remind the city that at that hour on Friday the second day of January in the year 1492, Spanish Islam departed into the silence of history.

When you arrive at the Alhambra, you will find that your coming has been exhaustively prepared for. Instructions, maps, detailed explanations and guides are present in profusion. The Alhambra is the rarest piece of architecture in the West—also a great and moving moment caught in stone. The best that can be done here, perhaps, is to describe briefly the plan and architecture, and then to indicate a route through the palace that will not cause you to retrace your steps too often.

The plan is distinctly Arab: plain exterior walls around an open courtyard dominating the rooms grouped about it. The Alhambra is nothing more than a series of such units.

A great deal of the beauty of the palace lies in its decoration. This ornament is achieved in three materials: wood, used in very small pieces; glazed and colored tile; and plaster. The plaster was decorated in two ways: by carving it while it was still wet, or by stamping it or molding it in that state—a later, easier and less satisfying method.

Begin your tour of the Alhambra by ignoring—for the moment, at any rate—the Renaissance palace of Charles I. The modern entrance takes you first to the *Patio de la Alberca* or *de los Arrayanes*—the Pool of the Myrtles, where fancy places the swimming pool for the gorgeous odalisques of the harem. Next is the *Sala de la Barca,* with its extraordinary stalactite arch. See the room in the *Torre de Gomares* where Boabdil and his chiefs resolved upon the surrender of Granada, and which has a most beautiful example of intricate wooden decoration in its ceiling, and some one hundred and fifty different designs stamped in the plaster. Go through the *Sala de los Mozárabes* to the famous *Patio de los Leones,* the Court of the Lions, elegantly beautiful, although the lions never roared in any jungle. The *Sala de los Abencerrajes* has a most impressive stalactite dome and a charming fountain, but no truth whatever in the legend the guide tells you about its being the hall where Boabdil cut off the heads of fifty rebellious lords. The *Sala de los Reyes,* the Hall of the Kings, has stalactite arches and honeycomb ceiling. The *Sala de Dos Hermanas,* the Two Sisters (thought to be the winter quarters of the harem), has a dome that is the perfection of the honeycomb style. Pass through the *Mirador de Daraxa,* and then back through the *Patio de los Leones* and the *Patio de los Arrayanes* and down to the *Patio del Mexuar* and the *Mexuar* itself, the Council Room. The beautiful façade of the *Cuarto Dorado,* the Guilded Room, is original, but the inside decoration is 16th century. The *Patio de Daraxa,* modern, but on the site of the original palace garden, has a charming fountain and cypress trees. In the adjoining apartments (called the *Aposentos de Carlos V,* Charles V's Lodgings), Washington Irving lived for several months, writing *The Alhambra.* You will go through the *Patio de la Reja,* with another fountain

Entrance to Court of the Lions

Garden of the Generalife, Alhambra Palace

Iron work (reja) in a chapel of San Nicolás in Úbeda; Courtyard of the town hall in Úbeda

and more cypresses, to the *Baño Real,* the Royal Baths; and from there to the *Torre del Peinador* and upstairs to the beautiful *Peinador de la Reina,* the Queen's Dressing Room.

In the gardens, the *Jardines del Partal,* stands the *Torre de las Damas,* with a beautiful upper room and a fine view. Two other towers have exquisitely decorated rooms: the *Torre de la Cautiva,* the Tower of the Captive (female), and the *Torre de las Infantas,* the Tower of the King's Daughters.

At the southern end of the Jardines del Partal is the convent of *San Francisco,* once a Moorish palace and now the national *albergue* where, it is to be hoped, you are staying.

In the 19th century the town fathers tore down hundreds of Arab houses and drove streets recklessly through all the ancient quarters. As a consequence, the Moorish remains are few. Among these: the *Casa del Carbón,* the Charcoal House, once a true Eastern "Caravanserai," an inn for travelers and merchants and also a warehouse for their goods; the *Ermita de San Sebastián,* the only *morabit,* or place of prayer, left from Moslem times; and the remains of Arab houses at No. 27, *Carrera del Darro,* and at No. 1, *Calle de Ceniceros,* in the Albaicín quarter.

Inevitably, at Granada, there are the gypsies in the caves of **Sacrononte.** They are popular with tourists, but for many people, difficult to take—and absurdly expensive, too. Their "native" manners, their singing and *flamenco,* seem to be the result of shrewd observation of four or five generations of the way foreigners expect a gypsy to sing, dance and behave.

On the outskirts of the city is the *Cartuja,* the Charterhouse. Brace yourself and go. You have never really disbelieved your eyes until you take your first look at the *Sacristía.* Inconceivable skill and some thirty years were put into the work—and the upshot is a dizzy, staggering intoxication of architecture. The Sacristy is Baroque on the bender of a lifetime. But you must see it.

GRANADA TO ÚBEDA AND BAEZA

From Granada you go north almost to **Jaén** and then northwest to **Úbeda.** Until lately, both Úbeda and its close kin, Baeza have been ignored, just as Zamora and Ciudad Rodrigo were. But Úbeda is a fine and unique mixture of Andalucía and Castile. The narrow, intertangled streets (By no means sally out from the parador by yourself on your first visit; two blocks away, and you're lost), the pebble paving, the whitewashed houses, the golden-colored walls, the Arab gate, called the *puerta de la Rosal,* the fountains surrounded by thirsty burros, and the patios of the houses—all this is *andaluz.* But the air is brisk, clear and cool, and the surrounding mountains, over six thousand feet tall, have the austerity and grandeur of Castile. Finally, there are the seignioral houses, built of golden-yellow stone, which speak of Salamanca rather than of the Alhambra.

Úbeda's history is eventful. Phoenicians, Greeks, Carthaginians, Romans, Vandals and Visigoths were all there. But the city owes most to the Renaissance, when it was splendidly furnished with great palaces —mainly the work of one admirable local architect, Andrés de Vandaelvira, who called in the great iron-masters of Spain to execute the superb iron work, *rejas,* for the churches of *Santa María de los Reales Alcázares, El Salvador* and *San Nicolás.*

The most resplendent part of the city is the square, the *plaza de Vázquez de Molina,* where you will be quartered in the palace of the

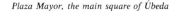

Plaza Mayor, the main square of Úbeda

Castle of Marques de Camarasa in Canena

Ortegas, a distinguished and grand building now serving as the Parador Nacional Condestable Dávalos.

You have been warned about losing yourself in the labyrinth of streets. But fortunately the *concierge* can find an intelligent man to serve you as guide. In his excessive enthusiasm he will undoubtedly walk your feet off, but in this most distinguished and elegant city you will have seen:

El Salvador, at one end of the beautiful plaza. Turn the corner for a sight of the handsome, two-storied and arcaded gallery that is part of the 16th-century Old People's Home, locally known as *Los Viejos de Salvador.*

Santa María de los Reales Alcázares, on the south side of the square, for the sake of its *reja.*

The excellently restored palace of Juan de Vázquez de Molina—he was Philip II's secretary—known now as the *Casa de las Cadenas,* or the *Ayuntamiento,* the Town Hall.

San Nicolás, for its *reja.*

San Pablo, near your plaza, for its general charm.

The *Hospital de Santiago,* a piece out of Herrera's book.

And a few, at least, of the houses: the *Casa del Conde de Guadiana,* which has a fine Renaissance angle tower; the *Palacio de Vela de los Cobos;* the *Casa de los Salvajes,* the House of the Wood Men, so called because of the shaggy creatures carved above the portal; and the plateresque *Casa de Díaz Madrid.*

Another impressive visit: From Úbeda northeast 31 kms. to Villacarrillo, then south to Peal de Becerro. Here you must make inquiries, because the way is difficult to find. You will end up following a dusty country road that winds up to the top of a hill past a white house—

and ends. A hundred yards away are the modern steps that go down into the *Cámara Sepulcral,* the Burial Chamber, dating from the 6th century B.C., the underground tomb of an Iberian chief of the city of Tugia, which lies beneath you. There is something oddly moving about these five little chambers—a strong sense of primitive man groping for skill in the trick of expressing himself through his arts. You will see an early fumbling for the shape of the true arch, an attempt at decorative moldings and, most touching of all, very shallowly incised capitals on the door jambs of the room where the chief's body was placed. Some stonecutter had traveled to Ampurias or Tartessos, perhaps, and had come back with something to imitate.

This whole area is filled with visible evidences of venerability. **Baeza,** 9 kms. west of Úbeda, is Iberian in its foundations. At the battlemented gates you come upon the *Fuente de los Leones,* the Lions' Fountain, which seems to supply at least a quarter of the city with its water. Surmounting the unreal but stanchly spouting lions is a statue thought to be of Cybele, though it may be of Imilce, the wife of Hannibal. In any event, it dates from pre-Roman antiquity.

The architecture of Baeza is as elegant and the ancestral houses are as numerous as those of Úbeda. But Baeza is gray; only on the west side have the buildings mellowed into an approximation of Úbeda's golden masonry.

Street and whitewashed walls of Úbeda   *Doorway of a palace in Baeza*

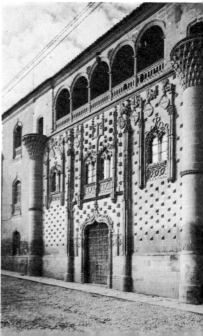

A dolmen, burial mound, near Antequera

Lose yourself in the network of narrow gray streets. You will find palace after palace hiding there, each with its heavy armorial bearings, and even a tower, now and again.

Not everything is ghostly in Baeza. Beside the two gates is the *Casa del Pópulo,* a charming Italianesque palace with a graceful colonnaded loggia. The church of *San Andrés,* which is early 16th century, has an elegant Renaissance portal. The *Seminario* is late Gothic, done in a Spanish-Flemish manner. (Don't fail to see the delightful patio.) The *town hall,* built in the mid-16th century, possesses a facade that is among the best of its style in Spain. And finally there is the entirely charming—and entirely dry—*fountain of St. Mary* in front of the cathedral, its eight paired columns standing in a four-lobed basin and supporting a little three-arched memorial to Charles I.

From Baeza you turn northwest to Linares and the main route north, N4, where you climb the steep pass out of Andalucía, the *Desfiladero de Despeñaperros,* a name which does not translate gracefully: The Pass of the Hurling of the Dogs over the Cliff. The cliff was the steep descent into the Moorish south, and the dogs, of course, were those infidels.

And at once you are back on the Central Meseta of the Castillas, in the famous region of La Mancha, with its vast gray and amber plains. La Mancha seems desiccated, though it does produce great quantities of wine and olive oil. But vines and olive trees are salamanders; they live in the invisible fire of the calcined soil and like it.

And so, some 160 kms. north of Baeza, in the middle of desiccation, you come to **Almagro,** without exaggeration one of the most delightful little towns in Spain. The Romans called it Mariana, after the wealthy Spaniard, Sextus Marius, who owned a huge tract of land hereabouts

Zamora from across the Duero River

until Tiberius took it for its gold and copper and had its owner flung down from the Tarpeian Rock. The town acquired a certain standing internationally when, in the 16th century, the Augsburg bankers, the Fuggers, built a palace there for the easier supervision of the *Campo de Calatrava*—which was in pledge to them for years because of bankrupt Charles I's borrowings.

Until 1936 Almagro had survived largely intact, but the violence of the first months of the Civil War bore heavily on it. Scarcely a public building went undamaged. Yet if you are there at the end of August, when the people have given the town its annual coat of whitewash and have polished all the windows in preparation for the great mule fair, you will find few traces of the damage. Almagro has a delicate, spacious Spanish quality. The *plaza mayor* is uncommonly large for so modest a town. The *paseo,* paved with river pebbles set in simple patterns, is flanked by flower beds and shrubbery. At the far end stands the 17th-century town hall. The other sides are lined with stone columns supporting an unbroken line of green-trimmed, glass-enclosed galleries. On the south side of the square is something of a rarity, the *Corral de Comedias,* the only intact 16th-century theater in Spain.

Away from the *plaza mayor* clean streets lead out, interrupted here and there by the brisk green of smaller squares. The town houses are, with one exception, not very large, but quietly handsome, and through the open doors of almost every one you look into the cool green and flowered light of a patio. But in the *calle de Nuestra Señora de las Nieves* stands a rather larger house. It belongs, the people will tell you, to the Marqués de Fúcar—the Fuggers of Augsburg.

And then from Almagro to Madrid, 233 kilometers . . . and so home.

CHAPTER *6*

SPANISH

Spanish, like English, is spoken in so many parts of the world that any linguistic unity is virtually impossible to achieve. Although you will find that pronunciation and spelling vary in different regions of Spain itself, do not let this deter you from the pleasure of speaking some Spanish. It is not only the courteous thing to do, but you may find it almost imperative in some of the less-traveled parts of Spain.

What follows is a brief guide to the pronunciation of Spanish and selected phrases and words to help you on your visit. You will notice that the Spanish use an inverted question mark at the beginning of a question, as well as the conventional one at the end.

PRONUNCIATION

Vowels: With a few exceptions, the five vowel sounds are as follows: *a*(*fa*ther), *e*(*wei*gh), *i*(m*ee*t), *o*(kn*o*w), *u*(tr*u*e). One variation is *u* in the syllable *gue* (gay) and *qui* (key). In diphthongs, *i* and *u* are not accented unless so indicated: río (ree-o).

Consonants: *c* as *k* except when followed by *e* or *i,* then the *c* is lisped: *ce*ra (*thay*-ra); *z* is always lisped: *za (thah);* in Castilian Spanish *b* is pronounced like *v* in *v*ery; *h* is always silent; *g* as in *g*ood except before *e* or *i,* when it is pronounced like the German *ch* or a strong English *h;* *m* and *n* are always detached: a*n*-gu-las; *l* as in will; *ñ* as in ca*ny*on; *r* is always rolled; *s* and *t* are always hard.

USEFUL PHRASES

Please	*por favor*	pohr fah*vo*hr
Thank you	*muchas gracias*	*moo*chas *grah*theeahs
You're welcome	*de nada*	day n*ah* dah
Good morning	*buenos días*	*bway*nohs *dee*ahs
What time is it?	*¿Qué hora es?*	kay *oh*ra ays
Excuse me	*perdón*	pair*dohn*
How are you?	*¿Cómo está usted?*	kohmoh ay*stah* oo-staydth

Windmills near Ciudad Real

Goodbye	*adiós*	ahdeeohs
Is it ready?	*¿Está listo?*	ais*tah lees*toh
What's that?	*¿Que es eso?*	kay ays *ay*soh
What's the matter?	*¿Que pasa?*	kay *pah*sah
Where is. . . .	*¿Dónde está. . . .*	*don*day ays*tah*
What do you want?	*¿Que quiere usted?*	kay *keeay*ray oo*staydth*
I want, wish	*Quiero, deseo*	*keeay*roh, day*sayoh*
With pleasure	*con mucho gusto*	kohn *moo*choh *goos*toh
It is good (bad) weather.	*Hace buen (mal) tiempo*	*ah*thay bwayn (mahl) *teeaym*poh
No smoking	*se prohibe fumar*	say prohee*bay* foo*mahr*
I don't understand	*no comprendo*	noh com*pren*doh

Is there someone here who speaks English?
¿Hay alguien aquí que hable inglés?
Ay ahl*geeain* ah*key* kay *ah*blay een*glays?*

AT THE HOTEL

Have you a single (double) room with (without) bath for the night?
¿Tiene usted una habitación para una sola persona (para dos personas) con (sin) baño para la noche?
*Teeay*nay oo*staydth oo*nah ahbeetah*theeohn pah*rah *oo*nah *soh*lah payr*soh*nah (*pah*rah dohs payr*soh*nahs) kohn (seen) *bahn*yo *pah*rah lah *noh*chay?

How much does it cost?
¿Cuánto cuesta?
*Kwan*toh kwes*tah?*

I like it (don't like it).
Me gusta (no me gusta).
May *goo*stah (noh may *goo*stah).

Is there a restaurant (garage)?
¿Hay un restaurante (gareje)?
Ay oon raystoh*rahn*tay (gah*rah*hay)?

When is the dining room open?
¿A que hora se abre el comedor?
Ah kay *oh*rah say *ah*bray ell kohmay*dohr?*

You may bring down my luggage.
Puede bajar el equipaje.
*Pway*day bah*har* ell aykey*pah*hay.

How much do I owe you?
¿Cuánto le debo?
*Kwahn*toh lay *day*boh?

Please let me have the bill.
Tenga la bondad de darme la cuenta.
*Tain*gah lah bohn*dahd* day *dahr*may lah *kwayn*tah

I'm in a hurry.
Tengo prisa.
*Tain*goh *pree*sah.

It's very important.
Es muy importante.
Ais mwee eempor*tahn*tay.

Please wake me at eight o'clock tomorrow morning.
Hágame el favor de despertame a las ocho mañana.
*Ah*gahmay ail fah*vohr* day dayspair*tahr*may ah lahs *oh*choh mahn*ya*na.

ON THE ROAD

Is this the road for . . . ?
¿Es ésta la carretera de . . . ?
Ais ais*tah* lah cahray*tay*rah day . . . ?

Is it far from here? How far (in point of time)?
¿Es lejos de aquí? ¿Cuánto tiempo?
Ais *lay*hos day ah*key*? *Kwahn*toh tee*aim*poh?

Straight ahead, to the left, to the right.
Todo seguido, a la izquierda, a la derecha.
*Toh*doh say*ghee*doh, ah lah eeth*keeair*dah, ah lah day*ray*chah.

Is the road in good condition?
¿Es buena la carretera?
Ais *bway*nah lah cahrav*tay*rah?
N.B. When a Spaniard calls a road—or anything else—"corriente," he doesn't mean "current" or "just ordinary"; he means "bad."

Can we get through this way?
¿Se puede pasar por aquí?
Say *pway*day pah*sahr* pohr ah*key*?

Please fill up the gas tank.
Llene usted el depósito por favor.
*Lyay*nay oo*staydth* ell day*poh*seetoh pohr fahvohr.

The Royal Palace in Madrid

I don't know what's the matter with the car.
No sé qué pasa con el coche.
Noh say kay *pah*sah kohn ell *koh*chay.

The motor doesn't work.
No funciona el motor.
Noh foon*theeown*ah ell moh*tohr.*

When can you return it, have it back?
¿Cuando puede devolverlo?
*Kwahn*doh *pway*day dayvohl*vair*loh?

How far is the next gas station?
¿Está muy lejos la gasolinera?
Ais*tah* mwee *lay*hohs lah gasonlee*nair*ah?

VOCABULARY

Note. Nouns followed by *m* (masculine) should be preceded by *el* (the); *f* (feminine) by *la*. If a feminine noun begins with a vowel, use *el*. The letter *v* indicates that the word is being used here as a verb.

Numbers

0 *cero*	*thay*roh	16 *diez y seis*	*dee*ayth ee *say*ees
1 *uno*	*oo*noh	17 *diez y siete*	*dee*ayth ee *seeay*-tay
2 *dos*	dohs		
3 *tres*	trayce	18 *diez y ocho*	*dee*ayth ee *oh*choh
4 *cuatro*	*kwah*troh	19 *diez y nueve*	*dee*ayth ee *nway*-vay
5 *cinco*	*theen*ko		
6 *seis*	*say*ees	20 *veinte*	*vayn*tay
7 *siete*	*seeay*tay	30 *treinta*	*trayn*tah
8 *ocho*	*oh*choh	40 *cuarenta*	kwah*rayn*tah
9 *nueve*	*nway*vay	50 *cincuenta*	theen*kwain*tah
10 *diez*	*dee*ayth	60 *sesenta*	say*sayn*tah
11 *once*	*own*thay	70 *setenta*	say*tayn*tah
12 *doce*	*doh*thay	80 *ochenta*	oh*chayn*tah
13 *trece*	*tray*thay	90 *noventa*	noh*vayn*tah
14 *catorce*	kah*tohr*thay	100 *cien*	thee*ayn*
15 *quince*	*keen*thay		

Months of the year

January	*enero*	*aynay*roh
February	*febrero*	fay*bray*roh
March	*marzo*	*mahr*thoh
April	*abril*	ah*breell*
May	*mayo*	*mah*yoh
June	*junio*	*hoon*eeoh
July	*julio*	*hool*eeoh
August	*agosto*	ah*gos*to
September	*septiembre*	sayp*teeaym*bray
October	*octubre*	ohk*too*bray
November	*noviembre*	noh*veeaym*bray
December	*diciembre*	dee*theeaym*bray

Las Palmas in the Canary Islands and its harbor

Days of the week

Sunday	*domingo*	doh*meen*go
Monday	*lunes*	*loo*nays
Tuesday	*martes*	*mahr*tays
Wednesday	*miércoles*	meeayr*kol*ays
Thursday	*jueves*	*hway*vays
Friday	*viernes*	veeayr*nays*
Saturday	*sábado*	*sah*bahdo

The car

Air	*aire* (m)	*ahee*ray
Battery	*acumulador* (m)	ahkoomoolah*dohr*
Brakes	*frenos (los)*	*fray*nohs (lohs)
Breakdown	*avería* (f)	ahvay*ree*ah
Broken	*roto*	*roh*toh
Clutch	*embrague* (m)	aim*brah*gay
Gasoline	*gasolina* (f)	gahsoh*leen*ah
Gears	*engranaje* (m)	aingrah*nah*hay
Liter	*litro* (m)	*lee*troh
Mechanic	*mecánico* (m)	may*kah*neekoh
Oil	*aceite* (m)	ah*thayee*tay
Puncture	*pinchazo* (m)	peen*chah*thoh
Radiator	*radiador* (m)	rahdeeah*dohr*
Regulate	*ajustar*	ahhoos*tahr*
Tighten	*apretar*	ahpray*tahr*
Tire	*neumático*	nayoo*mah*teekoh

General

Any	*algún*	ahl*goon*
Arrive	*llegar*	lyay*gahr*
At once	*en seguida*	ayn say*ghee*dah
Bad	*malo*	*mah*loh
Baggage	*equipaje* (m)	aykee*pah*hay
Bank	*banco* (m)	*bahn*koh
Bathroom	*cuarto de baño* (m)	*kwahr*toh day *bahn*yoh
Better	*mejor*	may*hohr*
Beautiful	*bello*	*bay*lloh
Bed	*cama* (f)	*kah*mah
Big	*grande*	*grahn*day
Bill	*cuenta* (f)	*kwayn*tah
Bottle	*botella* (f)	boh*tayl*lah
Boy	*chico* (m)	*chee*koh
Breakfast	*desayuno* (m)	daysah*yoo*noh

A typical town square, this one in Medina del Campo

Bring	*traer*	trah*ayr*
Carry	*llevar*	lyay*vahr*
Cheap	*barato*	bah*rah*toh
Church	*iglesia* (f)	ee*glay*seeah
Cigarette	*cigarrillo* (m)	theegahr*reel*yoh
Close (v)	*cerrar*	thayr*rahr*
Coffee	*café* (m)	kah*fay*
Cold	*frío*	*free*oh
Come	*venir*	vay*neer*
Concierge	*conserje* (m)	kohn*sayr*hay
Cup	*taza* (f)	*tah*thah
Dinner	*cena* (f)	*thay*nah
Double	*doble*	*doh*blay
Doctor	*médico* (m)	*may*deekoh
Drink (v)	*beber*	bay*bayr*
Drugstore	*farmacia* (f)	fahr*mah*theeah
Early	*temprano*	taym*prah*noh
Eat	*comer*	koh*mayr*
Elevator	*ascensor* (m)	ahsthain*sohr*
Expensive	*caro*	*kah*roh
Fast	*rápido*	*rah*peedoh
Film	*pelicula* (f)	pay*lee*koolah
First	*primero*	pree*may*roh
Floor	*piso* (m)	*pee*soh
Girl	*chica* (f)	*chee*kah
Give	*dar*	dahr
Glass	*vaso* (m)	*vah*soh
Go	*ir*	eer
Good	*bueno*	*bway*noh
Heavy	*pesado*	pay*sah*doh
Here	*aquí*	ah*kee*
Hospital	*hospital* (m)	ohspee*tahl*
Hot	*caliente*	kah*leeayn*tay
Hotel	*hotel* (m)	oh*tayl*
Ill	*enfermo*	ayn*fayr*moh
In	*en*	ayn
Late	*tarde*	*tahr*day
Less	*menos*	*may*nohs
Lunch	*almuerzo*	ahl*mooayr*thoh
Magazine	*revista* (f)	ray*vees*tah
Maid	*criada* (f)	*kreeah*dah
Match	*fósforo* (m)	*fohs*fohroh
Me	*me*	may

Menu	menú (m)	maynoo
Milk	leche (f)	laychay
Miss	señorita	saynyohreetah
Mr.	señor	saynyor
Mrs.	señora	saynyorah
More	más	mahs
Much	mucho	moochoh
Museum	museo (m)	moosayoh
My	mi	mee
Near	cercano	thayrkahnoh
Newspaper	periódico (m)	payreeohdeekoh
No	no	noh
Now	ahora	ahohrah
Open (adj.)	abierto	ahbeeayrtoh
Paper	papel (m)	pahpayl
Policeman	policía (f)	pohleetheeah
Porter	mozo (m)	mohthoh
Post office	correo (m)	kohrrayoh
Ready	listo	leestoh
Restaurant	restaurante (m)	raystohrahntay
See	ver	vayr
Send	enviar	aynveeahr
Soap	jabón (m)	hahbohn
Show	mostrar	mohstrahr
Single	sencillo	sentheeleeoh
Slow	lento	layntoh
Slowly	despacio	dayspahtheeo
Small	pequeño	paykaynyoh
Stamp	sello (m)	sayllyoh
Store	tienda (f)	teeayndah
Street	calle (f)	kahllyay
Strong	fuerte	fooayrtay
Suitcase	maleta (f)	mahlaytah
Taxi	taxi (m)	tahksee
Telephone	teléfono (m)	taylayfohnoh
Tip	propina	prohpeenah
Toilet	retrete (m)	raytraytay
Too	también	tahmbeeayn
Toothpaste	pasta dentífrica (f)	pahstah dayntee-freekah
Wait (for)	esperar	ayspayrahr
Waiter	camarero (m)	kahmahrayroh
Water	agua (f)	ahgwah
Weak	débil	daybeel
When	cuando	kwahndoh
Where	donde	dohnday
Who	quien	keyayn
Why	por qué	pohr kay
Wine	vino (m)	veenoh
Worse	peor	payohr
Yes	sí	see
Your	su	soo

CHAPTER 7

The section that follows is intended primarily as a brief guide to hotels and restaurants in the cities and larger towns of Spain. They are arranged alphabetically by town. In addition, addresses that might be useful to the tourist and some brief shopping information has been given where it seemed pertinent.

HOTELS

For convenience the hotels listed are identified in this section by one of the following symbols:

Five Stars (*****): Single, $76; Double, $106. (Breakfast, $6.50; Lunch or Dinner, $27) *Four Stars* (****): Single, $39; Double, $59. (Breakfast, $2.50; Lunch or Dinner, $11) *Three Stars* (***): Single, $25; Double, $37. (Breakfast, $1.60; Lunch or Dinner, $7.50) *Two Stars* (**): Single, $16; Double, $25. (Breakfast, $1.50; Lunch or Dinner, $6.50) One Star (*): Single, $12; Double, $19. (Breakfast, $1.20; Lunch or Dinner, $4).

Note: These are broad approximations intended to serve only as a general guide. In some areas rates may increase by as much as 15% during high season.

There are some hotels officially designated as Five Star-Gran Lujo (*****G.L.) category, such as the super-luxury Ritz, Madrid and the Los Monteros in Marbella, where prices for a double start at approximately $230, breakfast $10 and lunch or dinner $45.

The system of symbols used to characterize the hotels is also applied to the restaurants listed in this section.

****Superior restaurants charge $30 or $40 for lunch or dinner.
***Medium-high restaurants charge about $15 to $30 for lunch or dinner.
**Medium-priced restaurants charge from $10 to $15 for lunch or dinner.
*Inexpensive restaurants charge from $6 to $10 for lunch or dinner.
An average price anywhere for a continental breakfast (coffee, rolls, honey) is about $1.50. The initials T.I.O. stand for Tourist Information Office.

Albacete (Pop. 117,126)

HOTELS: ***Hotel Parador Nacional de la Mancha, Carretera Nacional 301, km. 260. 70 rooms. Country setting, tennis pool. ****Los Llanos, Avenida Espana 9. 102 rooms. On lovely city park.

RESTAURANTS: **Meson Las Rejas, Dionisio Guardiola 7. **Nuestro Bar, Alcalde Conangla 102. Excellent regional specialties.

Algeciras (Pop. 86,042)

HOTELS: ****Reina Cristina, Paseo de la Conferencia. 135 rooms. Beautiful garden and terrace, splendid view of Gibraltar. ****Hotel Octavio, San Bernardo 1. 80 rooms.

RESTAURANTS: **Marea Baja, Trafalgar 2. **El Grillo, Carretera N-340, km. 100. Popular meeting spot. (Both closed Sundays).

Alicante (Pop. 251,387)

HOTELS: ****Melia-Alicante, Playa del Postiguet. 545 rooms. ***Hotel Cavadonga, Plaza de los Luceros 17. 83 rooms. ****Gran Sol, Avda. Mendez Nunez 3. 150 rooms. *****Hotel Sidi San Juan Palace-Sol, Partida Cabo la Huerta. 176 rooms. On the beach.

RESTAURANTS: **Quo Vadis, Pl. Santisima Faz 3. Rustic atmosphere. ***Delfin, Esplanada de Espana 12. Best seafood in town.

Andraitx (Pop. 6,336)

HOTEL: ***Mini Folies, Cala Llamp (Mallorca). 54 rooms.

Antequera (Pop. 35,171)

HOTEL: ***Parador Nacional de Anteguera, 55 colorful rooms, Andalusian atmosphere and cuisine.

Aranda de Duero (Pop. 27,598)

HOTEL: ***Los Bronces. 29 rooms. On the old highway, tranquil with good service.

RESTAURANT: ***Meson de la Villa, Plaza Mayor. Famous for roast lamb (cordero asado).

Avila (Pop. 41,735)

HOTELS: ***Parador Nacional Raimundo de Borgona. Marques de Carnales y Chozas 16. 62 rooms. Magnificent 15th century palace. ****Gran Hotel Palacio de Valderrabanos, Pl. de la Catedral 9. 73 rooms. Elegant. * Hotel Reina Isabel, Av. Jose Antonio 17. 44 rooms.

RESTAURANTS: **Meson del Rastro, Pl. Del Rastro 1. **Piquio, Estrada 4. Castillian cuisine, excellent tapas.

Badajoz (Pop. 114,361)

HOTEL: ****Gran Hotel Zurbaran, Paseo de Castelbar 6. 215 rooms. Best in town, pool, restaurant.

RESTAURANT: **Caballo Blanco, Av. General Rodrigro 7. Closed Sun. ** Los Gabrieles, Vicente Barrantes 21.

Bagur (Costa Brava) (Pop. 2,277)

HOTEL: ***Hotel Bonaigua,* Playa de Fornells, 47 rooms. ****Hotel Aigua-blava,* Playa de Fornells. 85 rooms. Beach resorts; open April–October. ****Parador Nacional Costa Brava,* 80 rooms, pool spectacular sea views.

RESTAURANT: ***Sa Punta,* Closed Jan. 15–Feb. 15.

Barcelona (Pop. 1,754,900)

HOTELS: *****Princess Sofía.* Pl. Papa Pio XII, 505 rooms. *****Avenida Palace,* Gran Vía, 605. 211 rooms. *****Diplomatic,* Pau Claris 122. 213 rooms. Central and modern, pool. ****Manila,* Ramblas 111. 210 rooms. Centrally located, air conditioned roof garden with fine view. *****HUSA Presidente,* Avinguda Diagonal 570. 161 rooms. A favorite and distinguished gathering spot. *****Ritz,* Gran Vía 668. 197 rooms. Longtime favorite of many visitors, a classic ****Arenas,* Capitán Arenas 20. 59 rooms. ***Balmoral,* Vía Augusta, 5. 94 rooms. Air conditioned, garage. ****Gran Hotel Cristina,* Avda. Diagonal 458. 123 rooms. ****Derby,* Loreto 21. 116 rooms. Quiet location, very good restaurant. ****Majestic,* Passeig de Gràcia, 70. 344 rooms. ****Colón,* Avenida Catedral, 7. 161 rooms. Opposite the Cathedral. ****Dante,* Mallorca, 181. 81 rooms. *****Gran Hotel Sarriá-Sol* Av. de Sarria. 50. 314 rooms. ***Oriente,* Ramblas, 45. 142 rooms. ***Ficus,* Mallorca, 163. 78 rooms. ***Hotel Tres Torres,* Calatrava 32. 56 rooms. ****Hotel Condes de Barcelona,* Passeig de Gràcia, 75. 100 rooms. Newly restored marvelous 19th-century Gaudí-style art nouveau building. *****Miramar Palace,* on Montjuich Hill. 65 suites. New and one of Europe's best. ***Regencia Colón,* Sagristans, 13–17. 55 rooms. A bargain, in the picturesque Gothic Quarter.

RESTAURANTS: *****Eldorado Petit,* Dolores Monserdá, 51. Prize-winning cuisine with the best of Catalán and Spanish dishes. *****Reno,* Tuset, 27. A Barcelona classic. ****Jaume de Provença,* Provenza, 88. ****Neichel,* Avda. de Pedralbes, 17-bis. Excellent seafood. ****Vía Veneto,* Ganduxer, 10 & 12. Elegant, and outstanding cuisine. ****Ara-Cata,* Doctor Ferrán, 33. Good Catalán dishes. ****Casa Chus,* Diagonal, 339. ****Casa Isidro,* Les Flors, 12. ****Casa Quirza* (Espulgas de Llobregat). ****El Túnel,* Ample, 33–35. ***Els Perols de L'Empordà.* Villaroel à 88. ***El Vell Sarriá,* Plaza de la Villa, 11. *** *El Gran Café,* Avinyó, 9. ***Medulio,* Principe de Asturias, 6. ***Brasserie Flo,* Junquera, 10.

The Barceloneta is an old quarter of the city, on the beach near the port filled with one excellent seafood restaurant after another, in all price ranges. Their fresh seafood is displayed at the entrances with artistic flair to attract customers. Most are right on the beach, with indoor and outdoor dining. The following are just a few: ****Aitor,* Carbonell, 5. *** *Can Majo,* Almirante Aixada, 23. *** *Can Solé,* San Carlos 4.

T.I.O.: Gran Vía des Corts Catalans, 658. Tel.: 301-7443. *American Express:* Paseo de Gracia, 101. Chaflan Roellon. Tel.: 217-0070. *U.S. Consulate General,* Vía Layetana, 33. Tel.: 319-9550. *Canadian Consulate,* Vía Augusta, 125, Atico 3A. Tel.: 209-0634.

Benidorm (Pop. 25,544)

HOTELS: *****Gran Hotel Delfín,* Playa de Poniente-La Cala. 87 rooms. Tennis, pool, on the beach. ****Los Dálmatas,* Estocolmo 4. 270 rooms. Garden, pool. ***Alameda,* Alameda 36. 68 rooms.

RESTAURANTS: ****Tiffany's,* Avda. Mediterraneo, 3. ***La Pérgola,* Acantilado-Edif. Coblanca, calle 25.

On cliff with fantastic view. Piano bar. ***L'Escargot,* La Palma 13. French food, intimate atmosphere.

Bilbao (Pop. 433,030)

HOTELS: *****Villa de Bilbao,* Gran Vía, 87. 142 rooms. ***Conde Duque,* Campo Volantín, 22. 67 rooms. ****Aránzazu,* Rodríguez Arias, 66. 173 rooms. ****Husa Carlton,* Plaza Federico Moyua, 2. 142 rooms.

RESTAURANTS: ****Guria,* Gran Vía, 66. Elegant with great Basque seafood. ***Victor,* Plaza Nueva, 2. Excellent bacalao. *T.I.O.,* Alameda Mazarredo, s/n. Tel.: 424-4819. *U.S. Consulate,* Avenida del Ejercito, 11-3. Tel.: 435-8300. *American Express:* Viajes Cafranga, ("Viaca") Alameda Recalde, 68. Tel. 431-2049.

Burgos (Pop. 156,449)

HOTELS: *****Landa Palace,* Carretera de Madrid-Irún, Km.236. 39 rooms. Elegant, with pool & garden. Member Relais et Chateaux. ****Condestable,* Vitoria, 8. 82 rooms. Good restaurant with Castillian food.

RESTAURANTS: ***Los Chapiteles* General Santocilde, 7. Fine Castillian cuisine. Closed Sundays. ***Casa Ojeda,* Vitoria, 5. Good tapas before dining.

Cáceres (Pop. 71,852)

HOTELS: ***Alcántara,* Avda. Virgen de Guadalupe, s/n. 67 rooms. ***Extremadura,* Avda. Virgen de Guadalupe, s/n. 68 rooms.

RESTAURANT: ***El Figón de Eustaquio,* Plaza de San Juan, 12. In town's monumental section. Regional cuisine.

Cadaqués (Pop. 1,547)

HOTELS: ***Llane Petit,* Playa Llane Petit, s/n. 35 rooms. On the beach, garden. ***Playa Sol,* Playa Pianch, 5. 49 rooms.

RESTAURANT: ***La Galiota,* Narciso Monturiol, 9. Small, pleasant, fresh seafood.

Cádiz (Pop. 157,766)

HOTELS: ***Atlántico,* Parque Genovés, 9. 173 rooms. Magnificent view of the bay. ***Regio,* Ana de Viya, 11. 40 rooms. ***Francia y París,* Plaza Calvo Sotelo, 2. 69 rooms. In center of town.

RESTAURANTS: ***El Faro,* San Félix, 15. Seafood specialties. ***El Anteojo,* Alameda Apodaca, 22. Andalusian cuisine and fritura (fried fish). ***Curro el Cojo,* Paseo Marítimo, 2. Good local ham and sausages.

Calpe (Pop. 8,000)

HOTEL: ***Paradero Ifach,* Explanada del Puerto, 50. 29 rooms. Beach, tennis.

RESTAURANTS: ***El Claustro,* Urb. La Cometa, 14.

Calviá (Mallorca) (Pop. 22,016)

HOTEL: ****Club Galatzo,* Urbanización Ses Rotes Velles. 198 rooms. (Open from April 1 to Oct. 31).

RESTAURANT: *C'An Pau Perdiueta,* Cotoner, 47. Run by traditional fishing family.

Castelldefels (Pop. 13,219)

HOTEL: ****Gran Hotel Rey Don Jaime,* Avda. del Hotel, s/n. 88 rooms. Tennis, garden, beach.

Ciudad Rodrigo (Salamanca) (Pop. 14,766)

HOTEL: ***Parador Nacional Enrique II,* Plaza del Castillo, 1. 27 rooms. In castle built into ancient city walls.

Córdoba (Pop. 284,737)

HOTELS: ****Parador Nacional la Arrazafa,* Avda. de la Arruzafa, s/n. 83 rooms. Modern, but built on 8th Century Moorish site. ****Meliá Córdoba, Jardines de la Victoria. 106 rooms. Luxurious.

RESTAURANTS: ***El Caballo Rojo, Cardinal Hierro, 28. An award winner. **Oscar, Plaza de los Chirinos, 6. Home cooking, fresh seafood. (Also, try the Cordovan specialties at the Parador).

Cuenca (Pop. 41,791)

HOTEL: ***Alfonso VIII, Parque de San Julián, 3. 48 rooms. Modern, comfortable.

RESTAURANTS: **Mesón de las Casas Colgadas, Canónigos, s/n. Situated right in one of the "hanging houses," good regional dishes.

Denia (Pop. 22,162)

HOTEL: ***Denia, Partida Suertes del Mar. 280 rooms. On beach, with garden & pool.

RESTAURANT: *el Pati de la Creu, charming, excellent fresh seafood, in picturesque old section.
El Escorial See: San Lorenzo de El Escorial.

Fuenterrabia (Pop. 11,276)

HOTEL: ***Parador Nacional El Emperador, Plaza de Armas del Castillo. 16 rooms. A historical castle visited by King Ferdinand and Queen Isabel.

RESTAURANT: ***Ramón Roteta, Villa Ainara, Irún s/n.

Gijon (Pop. 255,969)

HOTELS: ****Hernán Cortés, Fernandez Vallin, 5. 109 rooms. ***Robledo, Alfredo Truán, 2. 133 rooms.

RESTAURANT: **La Pondala, Avda. Dionisio Cifuentes, 27 (Somió). Traditional; roast beef & seafood.
T.I.O., General Vigón, 3. Tel.: 341-167.

Granada (Pop. 262,182)

HOTELS: ****Parador Nacional San Francisco, Alhambra. 35 rooms. Restored convent on the grounds of the Alhambra. ****Alhambra Palace, Peña Partida, 2. 121 rooms. Magnificent view. ***Guadalupe, Avda. de los Alijares, s/n. 43 rooms.

RESTAURANTS: ***Ruta de Veleta (Cenes de la Vega, 5 km.) Country setting. **Baroca, Pedro Antonio de Alarcón, 34. Good venison dishes. * Suspiro del Moro, (Otura, 14 km.) Regional dishes.
T.I.O., Pavaneras, 19. Tel.: 221022. American Express, Viajes Aymar, S.A., Angel Ganivet, 2.

Gredos (Pop. 611)

HOTEL: ***Parador Nacional de Gredos. 77 rooms. Mountain hunting lodge near Avila; good game, trout, spectacular view.

Guadalupe (Pop. 2,765)

HOTEL: ***Parador Nacional Zurbarán, Marqués de la Romana, 10. 25 rooms. Converted convent with garden, pool.

RESTAURANT: **Hospedería del Real Monasterio, Plaza de Don Juan Carlos I. Good Extremadura regional dishes.

Jaen (Pop. 96,429)

HOTELS: ****Parador Nacional Castillo de Santa Catalina. 43 rooms. Modern, within an ancient castle. *** Xauen, Plaza de Deán Mazas, 3. 35 rooms.

RESTAURANT: **Mesón Nuyra, Pasaje Nuyra. Partridge and good wine cellar.

Javea (Pop. 10,964)

HOTEL: ****Parador Nacional Costa Blanca. 65 rooms. Magnificent beach location. Good typical rice dishes.

Jerez de la Frontera (Pop. 176,238)

HOTEL: *****Jerez, Avda. Alcalde Alvaro Domecq. 120 rooms. Tropical gardens, pool, excellent restaurant.

León (Pop. 131,134)

HOTELS: *****(Gran Lujo) *San Marcos.* 258 rooms. Absolutely magnificent 16th century monastery, now a Parador. ****Conde Luna,* Independencia, 7. 154 rooms.

RESTAURANT: ***Novelty,* Independencia, 4. Various excellent regional dishes.

Lugo (Pop. 73,986)

HOTELS: ****Gran Hotel Lugo,* Avda. Ramón Ferreiro s/n. 168 rooms. ***Méndez Núñez,* Reina, 1. 94 rooms.

RESTAURANT: ***Mesón de Alberto,* Cruz, 4. Galician dishes.

Madrid (Pop. 3,792,561)

The list below, arranged roughly according to price, ranges from *Gran Lux* establishments to modest and moderate-priced hotels. Like their counterparts elsewhere, the plush hotels are expensive. At the other end of the list you will find comfort without ostentation.

HOTELS: *****Barajas,* Avda. Logroño, 305. At Madrid International Airport. 230 rooms. Pool. Free transportation to terminals. ****Castellana,* Paseo de la Castellana 49. 313 rooms. A favorite of U.S. tourists. *****Eurobuilding,* Padre Damián 23. 420 rooms. Luxurious and well managed. *****Hotel Villa Magna,* Paseo de la Castellana 22. 194 rooms. Gran lux category and the epitome of elegance, taste, and service. *****Luz Palacio,* Paseo de la Castellana 57. 182 rooms. Near convention center. *****Meliá Madrid,* Princesa 27. 266 rooms. Located right on the Plaza de España. *****Monte Real,* Arroyo Fresno, 17. 77 rooms. Surrounded by wooded hills, close to the Puerto de Hierro Golf Club. *****Palace,* Plaza de las Cortes, 7. 517 rooms. One of Spain's great classic hotels, with a great location across the street from American Express and the Prado Museum. *****Ritz Madrid,* Plaza de la Lealtad, 5. Gran lux. 156 rooms. An aristocratic hotel in the grand manner, one of the best in Europe. Situated across the street from the Prado Museum. ****Plaza,* in the skyscraper "Edifico Espana," on the Plaza de Espana near Gran Via. 306 rooms. Roof garden restaurant. ** *Hotel Baltimore,* Bravo Murillo 160. 25 rooms. **Hotel Asturias,* Sevilla 2. 160 rooms. ****Sanvy,* Goya 3. 141 rooms. Recently renovated, pool & garden on roof. ****Suecia,* Marqués de Casa Riera 4. 64 rooms. Excellent central location. ****Gran Hotel Velázquez,* Velázquez 62. 130 rooms. Comfortable. *****Miguel Angel,* Miguel Angel 31. 304 Rooms. Ultra modern facilities, garden, pool, disco. *****Wellington,* Velázquez 8. 258 rooms. A favorite of celebrity bullfighters, in elegant shopping area. ****Emperador,* Gran Vía 53. 232 rooms. Excellent central location, pool. ****Holiday Inn Madrid,* Avenida General Perón s/n. 313 rooms. New, in Madrid's modern, chic and swinging Azca section. *** *Gran Hotel Victoria,* Plaza del Angel, 7. 110 rooms. In the heart of picturesque Old Madrid. *Residencia Hostal Lisboa,* Ventura de la Vega 17. 23 rooms. Private baths, pleasant, very well run, good location. Madrid's innumerable *pensiones* are not designed primarily for tourists, but should you decide to try one, a Tourist Information Office will help you in making a selection.

RESTAURANTS: *****Horcher,* Alfonso XII, 6. Superb European cuisine and wine cellar. By the Retiro Park. *****Jockey,* Amador de los Ríos, 6. Among Europe's finest. *****Zalacaín,* Alvarez de Baena, 4. (Relais-Gourmand) Possibly the best restaurant in Spain. *****Rue Royal,* Paseo de la Castellana, 22. In Madrid's gran

luxe Villa Magna Hotel. A gourmet's delight in elegant atmosphere. *****
Ritz, Madrid, Plaza de la Lealtad, 5. The elegant dining room of Madrid's aristocratic hotel. *****El Amparo,* Callejón de Puigcerdá, 8. Tastefully elegant. French-Basque cuisine. ****
Principe de Viana, Manuel de Falla, 5. Excellent Basque-Navarra menu. ****El Cenador del Prado,* Calle Prado, 4. Exquisite decor and food to match. ****Café de Oriente,* Plaza de Oriente. Friendly atmosphere. Royalty and ministers dine here, across from the Royal Palace. ****Casa Lucio,* Cava Baja, 35. Historical and typical, on one of Madrid's most fascinating streets in the old section. ***
Posada de la Villa, Cava Baja, 9. Founded in 1642, but in a new building on same street. ***Gure-Etxea,* Plaza de la Paja, 12. Basque cooking par excellence, on a square older than Madrid itself. ****El Estragón,* Plaza de la Paja, 10. Delightfully Spanish. ***Restaurante Plaza Mayor,* Gerona, 4. Alongside the Main Square, outdoor dining in spring and summer. **Taberna de Antonio Sánchez,* Mesón de Paredes, 13. One of Madrid's oldest and most authentic taverns. **Café Status,* Lagasca, 81. American food in delicious Spanish style, friendly atmosphere. **La Chata,* Cava Baja, 24. Roast suckling pig, lamb, tapas. ***La Gamella,* Calle de la Unión, 8. Owned by an American gourmet. Charming atmosphere. **Café Concierto,* Prado, 4. Soothing for tea, cocktails, and classical music. Near picturesque Plaza Santa Ana. **La Trucha,* Manuel Fernández y González, 3. Just off Plaza Santa Ana. Totally typical and terrific for tapas. *La Mi Venta,* Plaza Marina Española, 7. Big selection of excellent Tapas. In front of the Palacio del Senado. ***Antigua Casa Sobrino de Botín.* Founded in 1725. Very popular with tourists. *Mesón Museo del Jamón* (Ham museum).

Four locations: Carrera San Jerónimo, 6; Gran Vía, 72; Paseo del Prado, 44; Atocha, 54. Four thousand hams from four regions of Spain in each. Great sandwiches and snacks. *
El Corgo, Rollo, 8. Just down the steps from the tiny Plaza San Javier. Very good tapas and Galician food.

NIGHTLIFE: Madrid nightlife ranges from Los Vegas-style nightclub extravaganzas to *café conciertos. Scala Meliá Castilla,* Capitán Haya, 43. (In the Meliá Castilla Hotel building). Dinner, dancing, and spectacular reviews. The first show starts at 10:30 P.M. *Florida Park,* inside the Retiro Park (enter at Menéndez Pelayo at Ibiza street). Celebrity nightclub reviews, dinner, and dancing. Madrid has great *tablaos flamencos,* authentic flamenco performances. Among the best are: *Corral de la Morería,* Morería, 17; and *Café de Chinitas,* Torija, 7. Most *tablaos* open around 10 P.M. and drinking, dining, and dancing go on until 3 A.M. *El Casino de Madrid,* just out of town on the highway to La Coruña. Gambling, dining and nightclub shows. (Free transportation from downtown). For a great disco, try *Joy Eslava,* at Calle Arenal 11, next door to the Church of San Ginés. It's an old converted theater with great atmosphere. For a late night snack afterwards, go next door to the *Chocolatería San Ginés* for coffee or hot chocolate and *churros.* They open at 5 A.M. for the after-disco crowd. There is a new rage in Madrid: flamenco dancing at the discos. Some nightclubs, called *"salas rocieras"* are especially for folkloric fun and dancing Sevillanas, which is done in couples or groups. One of the best is *La Maestranza,* Mauricio Legendre, 16 (near the Chamartin Station). In addition to fine Andalusian cuisine, it features shows with outstanding Sevillana dancers, and those who know how are welcome to participate. To reserve a table, call 315-9059. A smaller informal *sala rociera* in a typical old Madrid neighborhood is *Las Marismas del Rocio,* Calatrava 6. In addition to shows, they offer Sevillanas classes.

SHOPPING: The two major department stores, with branches all over Spain, are *Galerías Preciados* and *El Corte Inglés.* They offer wide selections in men's and women's fashion, fine Spanish Lladró porcelains, Majórica Pearls, and Spanish handicrafts. They also have very good restaurants. Serrano street is lined with some of Europe's most elegant shops and boutiques. For fine leather fashions and accessories: *Loewe,* Serrano 16 and Gran Vía 8; also, *Lepanto,* Plaza de Oriente, 3. For fine Spanish handicraft: *Artespaña,* Plaza las Cortes, 3 (right near American Express). For a vast array of all types of interesting shops, stroll around the Plaza Mayor. While inside the square, look in at *Gritos de Madrid* at Plaza Mayor 6 for gift items and hand-painted ceramics. And for a most unusual shopping experience, be sure to visit the *Rastro Flea Market* on a Sunday Morning. It is located at Plaza Cascorro, deep in the old section of town. *Tourist Information Offices:* Duque de Medinaceli, 2. Tel.: 429-9274 (Province of Madrid); Plaza Mayor, 3. Tel.: 266-5477 (City of Madrid); Plaza España-Torre de Madrid. Tel.: 241-2325 (National Tourist Office of Spain). They also have offices at Madrid's Barajas Airport. *American Express,* Plaza de las Cortes, 2. Tel.: 429-5775. *U.S. Embassy,* Serrano, 75. Tel.: 276-3400. *Canadian Embassy,* Edificio Goya, Calle Núñez de Balboa, 35. Tel.: 431-4300.

Málaga (Pop. 503,251)

HOTELS: ******Málaga Palacio,* Cortina del Muelle, 1. 228 rooms. In the heart of town and near the port with every luxury. Pool. ****Parador Nacional de Gibralfaro.* 12 rooms. High above the city on the ruins of a moorish fortress. Spectacular view. Great for cocktails and dining. ***Casa Curro,* Sancha de Lara, 7. 105 rms. Centrally located.

RESTAURANTS: ***Antonio Martín,* Paseo Marítimo s/n. Terraced over the sea. Famous for "Málaga fish fry" *(fritura malagueña).* ***Casa Pedro,* Playa de El Palo, Quitapenas. Famous for sardines cooked on a spit *(espetón de sardinas),* typical in Málaga. During the warmer months, you can walk down the beach by the port to the *chiringuitos,* little open-air restaurants and stands where they cook fresh, skewered sardines over open fires.

Marbella (Pop. 67,822)

HOTELS: ******Meliá Don Pepe,* Finca Las Merinas. 218 rooms. Grand resort luxury on the Costa del Sol. G.L. ******Los Monteros,* Urb. Los Monteros, s/n. 171 rooms. (Relais et Chateaux). More luxury on the beach.

RESTAURANTS: ******La Hacienda,* Mediterranean excellence with an award-winning chef. ***La Virginia,* Camino de Camoján (across from the Meliá Don Pepe). Pleasant outdoor seating and good Andalusian dishes and home made desserts.

Mérida (Pop. 41,783)

HOTEL: *****Parador Nacional Vía de la Plata,* Plaza de la Constitucion, 3. 53 rooms. A converted 16th century convent. Also, has an excellent restaurant serving regional cuisine of Extremadura.

Olite (Pop. 2,829)

HOTEL: ****Parador Nacional Principe de Viana,* Plaza de los Teobaldos, 2. A grand 14th century castle. Just 28 miles south of Pamplona.

Oropesa (Pop. 3,069)

HOTEL: *****Parador Nacional Virrey Toledo.* 44 rooms. A splendid 14th century castle overlooking tranquil countryside and a quaint village. Luxurious rooms in medieval atmosphere. Their restaurant is excellent.

Oviedo (Pop. 190,123)

HOTEL: *****De la Reconquista, Gil de Jaz, 16. 139 rooms.

RESTAURANT: ****Trascorrales, Plaza Trascorrales, 18. Simple elegance and unforgettable Asturian cuisine.

Palma de Mallorca (Pop. 304,422)

HOTELS: *****Son Vida Sheraton, Urb. Sonuida, 13. 170 rooms. (Relais et Chateaux). Jet-set luxury in a converted 13th century hilltop castle. *****Valparaiso Palace, Francisco Vidal s/n. 138 rooms. Luxurious, with magnificent views of the bay. ****Uto Palma, Avda. Joan Miro 303. 234 rooms. Beach, pool. ***Palladium, Paseo Mallorca, 40. 53 rooms. Charming.

RESTAURANTS: ***El Gallo, Teniente Torres, 17. Great Mallorcan food. ****Violet, Zanglada, 2. Great seafood. **Rififi, Avda de Joan Miró, 186. Fish and shellfish.
T.I.O.: Avda. Jaime III, 10. Tel.: 21-22-16. American Express: Viajes Iberia, Es Born, 14. Tel.: 72-67-43.

Ronda (Pop. 31,383)

HOTELS: ****Reina Victoria, Jerez, 25. 89 rooms. Majestic view, great atmosphere.

RESTAURANTS: **Don Miguel, Villanueva, 4. Cliffhanging view. Good lamb and trout.

S'Agaró (Pop. 100)

HOTEL: G.L. *****Hostal de la Gavina, Plaza de la Rosaleda. 74 rooms. (Relais et Chateaux) Sophisticated resort on the Costa Brava.

RESTAURANT: ****La Gavina (at the hotel). Seaside elegance.

Salamanca (Pop. 167,131)

HOTELS: ****Parador Nacional de Salamanca, Teso de la Feria, 2. 108 rooms. High on a hill. Fine dining room.

RESTAURANTS: ***Chez Victor, Espoz y Mina, 26. The best in town. **La Posada, Aire, 1. Very popular; regional dishes.

San Lorenzo de El Escorial (Pop. 9,518)

HOTEL: ****Victoria Palace, Juan de Toledo, 4. 87 rooms. Pool, garden.

RESTAURANT: ***Charolés, Floridablanca, 24. Classic Castillian cuisine.

San Miguel (Ibiza) (Pop. 1,112)

HOTEL: ****Hacienda Na-Xamena. 54 rooms. Splendidly secluded luxury setting high above the Mediterranean. Excellent restaurant.

San Sebastián (Pop. 175,576)

HOTELS: *****María Cristina, Paseo República Argentina, s/n. 168 rooms. A classic. ****Londres y de Inglaterra, Zubeita, 2. 120 rooms. Beach.

RESTAURANT: ****Arzak, Alto de Miracruz, 1. (Relais-Gourmant). Elegant. **Casa Alkalde, Mayor, 19. Traditional Basque cuisine.
T.I.O.: Andía, 13. Tel.: 42-17-74.

Street scene, Santiago de Compostela

Santander (Pop. 180,328)

HOTELS: *****Real, Paseo de Pérez Galdós, 28. 124 rooms. Open during tourist season, July 1–September 15. ***Sardinero, Plaza de Italia, 113 rooms. On the main beach.

RESTAURANTS: ***La Sardina, Doctor Fleming, 3. Specialties of the Cantabrian Sea. **Posada del Mar, Juan de la Costa, 3. Very typical.

Santiago de Compostela (Pop. 93,695)

HOTELS: G.L. *****Reyes Católicos, Plaza de España, 1. 157 rooms. Magnificent and richly historical. ****Peregrino, Rosalía de Castro s/n. 148 rooms. Pool. **Hostal Vilas, Avda. Romera Donallo, 9. 28 rooms.

RESTAURANTS: ****Vilas, Rosalía de Castro, 88. Charming historical atmosphere. **Pampin, Puente Espiño. Calo Teo. Fresh seafood.
T.I.O.: Rúa del Villar, 43. Tel.: 58-40-81.

Santillana del Mar (Pop. 3,884)

HOTEL: ***Parador Nacional Gil Blas, Plaza Ramón Pelayo, 11. 28 rooms. A 15th-century converted mansion in the seaside mountains. The Altamira Cave is just 3 km. away. The restaurant features seafood specialties of the Cantabrian Sea.

Segovia (Pop. 53,237)

HOTELS: ****Parador Nacional de Segovia. 80 rooms. Splendid views of the city from this modern building of traditional architecture. Pool. ***Acueducto, Padre Claret, 10. 77 rooms. ***Puerta de Segovia, Ctra. Soria-Riaza. 100 rooms. Tennis, pool.

RESTAURANTS: ***José Maria, Cronista Lecea, 11. (Closed during November). Classic local dishes. **Casa Amado, Fernández Ladreda, 9. The best seafood in Segovia plus fine suckling pig. **Mesón de Cándido, Plaza del Azoguejo, 5. The interesting atmo-

sphere of an old inn at the foot of the Roman aquaduct.

Seo de Urgel (Pop. 10,681)

HOTELS: ***Parador Nacional Seo de Urgel. 85 rooms. In the heart of the old section. Restaurant features typical Catalonian dishes. ***Castell Motel, Ctra. Seo-Lérida. 39 rooms. (Relais et Chateaux).

RESTAURANTS: ***Castell Motel, at the hotel. Luxurious, exquisite salmon dishes. **Casa Dolcet, Avda. J. Zulueta, 1. Excellent home-style Catalonian dishes including crema catalana.

Seville (Pop. 653,883)

HOTELS: G.L. *****Alfonso XIII, San Fernando, 2. 149 rooms. Housed in an immense magnificent palace. Luxurious, spacious rooms, pool, central location. ****Colón, Canalejas, 1. 262 rooms. ****Doña María, Don Remondo, 19. 61 rooms. Right near the Giralda. Garden, pool. ****Los Lebreros, Luis de Morales, 2. 439 rooms. Next to El Corte Inglés, for good shopping.

RESTAURANTS: ****La Dorada, Virgen de Aguas Santas, 6. Authentically elegant, superb seafood and Andalusian cuisine and service to match. ***Figon del Cabildo, Plaza de Cabildo s/n. Typical Sevillian atmosphere and good regional cuisine. ***El Rincón de Curro. Virgen de Luján, 45. In the beautiful Remedios section. **La Albahaca, Plaza de Santa Cruz, 12. Rigit in the picturesque Santa Cruz quarter. **Mesón del Moro, Mesón del Moro, 6–10. In a beautiful 12th-century Moorish house. **Río Grande, Betis, s/n. Good view of the Giralda and the Torre del Oro from the banks across the Guadalquivir River in the picturesque Trana Quarter. ****Or-Iza, Betis, 61. Good Basque cuisine, also in Triana Quarter. ***Enrique Becerra, Gamazo, 2.

Lively atmosphere and good tapas. **
Casa Senra, Bécquer, 4. Popular with
bullfighters. Great gazpacho. ***La
Taberna Dorada*, José Luis de Caso,
18. Excellent seafood.

SHOPPING: The Calle de las Sierpes is
lined with shops which offer good
buys in leather, gloves, shoes, embroidery, handicrafts, and souvenir items.
Cerámica Santa Ana, across the river
in the Triana Quarter, is interesting
for hand-painted tiles and ceramics.
The *Corte Inglés* and *Galerías Preciados* department stores should be explored for good buys of all kinds.

T.I.O.: Avenida de la Constitución,
21. Tel.: 22-14-04 (Province of Seville); *Reales Alcázares*, Puerta del
León. Tel.: 22-95-74 (City of Seville).
American Express: Viajes Alhambra,
Teniente Coronel Segui, 6. Tel.: 22-
44-35.

Sitges (Pop. 11,850)

HOTELS: ***Calipolis*,   Paseo
Marítimo s/n. 179 rooms. Nice loca-
tion on the beach. ***Terramar*,
Paseo Marítimo, s/n. 209 rooms. Fac-
ing the sea. Tennis, golf, pool. Open
June 1–September 30.

RESTAURANT: ***El Greco*, Paseo de
la Ribera, 72. **La Masía*, Carretera
de Villanueva km 38. Catalonian
food.

Toledo (Pop. 57,769)

HOTELS: ****Parador   Nacional
Conde de Orgaz*, Paseo de los Cigar-
rales, s/n. On a hill overlooking the
city. Very much in demand. ***Carlos V*, Escalerilla de la Magdalena, 3.
55 rooms. ***Alfonso VI*, General
Moscardó, 2. 80 rooms.

RESTAURANTS: ***Hostal del Carde-
nal*, Paseo de Recaredo, 24. At the
entrance of the city. Good Castillian
dishes. ***Adolfo*, Granada 6. **La

Tarrasca, Hombre de Palo, 6. Good
tapas and regional dishes.

SHOPPING: Toledo shops feature jew-
elry, embroidery, ceramics, Spanish
costumes, and beautiful linens. The
National Arms Factory sells splendid
knives, daggers, and swords.
T.I.O., Puerta de Bisagra, s/n. Tel.:
22-08-43.

Torremolinos (Pop. 25,000)

HOTELS: *****Meliá Torremolinos*,
Avda Carlota Alessandri, 109. 283
rooms. *****Pez Espada*, Vía Impe-
rial. 147 rooms. ****Parador Nacional del Golf*. All three are on the
beach.

RESTAURANTS: ***Casa Guaquín*,
Carmen, 37. (Closed December) Fac-
ing the beach. Good seafood. **Antonio*, Playa del Remo (La Carihuela).
Good *fritura malagueña*. (Closed November)

Valencia (Pop. 751,734)

HOTELS: *****Sidi Saler Palace*,
Playa del Saler s/n. 272 rooms. Pool,
tennis, good beach location. ****
Parador Nacional Luis Vives, Ctra.
Saler, km. 16. 58 rooms. Beach loca-
tion, golf, fine dining room. ****
Reina Victoria, Barcas 4. 92 rooms.
***Oltra*, Plaza País Valencia, 4. 93
rooms.

RESTAURANTS: ****La Hacienda*,
Navarro Reverter, 12. Fine seafood
and paella, of course. ****Eladio*,
Chiva, 40. Great paella, seafood, and
salmon mousse. ****Ma Cuina*, Gran
Vía Germanías, 49. Great typical rice
dishes. **La Marcelina*, Avda. Nep-
tuno, 10. Good rice and seafood
dishes.
T.I.O.: Paz, 46. Tel.: 352-2897.
American Express: Viajes Meliá, Paz,
41. Tel.: 352-2642.

Valladolid (Pop. 320,242)

HOTELS: ****Felipe IV*, Gamazo, 16. 130 rooms. ****Olid Meliá*, Plaza de San Miguel, 10. 238 rooms. ***Meliá Parque*, Joaquín Garcí Morato, 17. 306 rooms.

RESTAURANTS: ****La Fragua*, Paseo de Zorilla, 10. Fine Castillian cuisine. ****Mesón Panero*, Marina Escobar, 1. ***Mesón Cervantes*, El Rastro, 6. **Bodega "La Sorbona"*, (Fuensaldaña, 8 km.). Castillian dishes and good house wine.

Zaragoza (Pop. 590,750)

HOTELS: *****Corona de Aragón*, Avda Cesar Agusto, 13. 251 rooms. *****Palafox*, Casa Jiménez s/n. 184 rooms. ****Rey Alfonso I*, Coso, 17–19. 117 rooms.

RESTAURANTS: ****Costa Vasca*, Teniente Coronel Valenzuela, 13. Outstanding Basque cuisine. ***Los Borrachos*, Paseo de Gagasta, 64. (Closed August). ***Mesón del Carmen*, Hernán Cortés, 4.

INDEX